# FORESTS
# FOR WHOM
# AND FOR
# WHAT?

# FORESTS FOR WHOM AND FOR WHAT?

Marion Clawson

Published for Resources for the Future, Inc.
by The Johns Hopkins University Press, Baltimore and London

Copyright © 1975 by The Johns Hopkins University Press
All rights reserved
Manufactured in the United States of America

Originally published, 1975

Johns Hopkins paperback edition, 1975
Second printing, 1976
Third printing, 1978
Fourth printing, 1984

Library of Congress Catalog Card Number 74-24399
ISBN 0–8018–1698–x (hardcover)
ISBN 0–8018–1751–x (paperback)

Library of Congress Cataloging in Publication data will be found on the last printed page of this book.

# Contents

# Tables

# Preface

This book is directed to the intelligent, interested nonspecialist—the person concerned about national policy for forests of all ownerships, all types, and all uses. It is not directed primarily toward the forester, the ecologist, the economist, or any other specialist, although hopefully each may find something of value here; its language and terminology have been chosen with its audience in mind. My purpose is to present facts and ideas and to introduce and discuss policy alternatives, including—as far as possible in a book of modest length—a consideration of who benefits and who loses from different policies. In the final chapter, I state my personal position on the major issues of forest policy, but I do not advocate or strive for the adoption of a program for forests of any specific ownership, type, or location. Hopefully, the facts and analyses presented will be helpful to the reader in his choice of the forest policy most desired by him.

At Resources for the Future, we have long had an interest in forests and forest policy. A review of our current list of publications or of our annual reports for the past several years will show many concrete examples of our general interest in the subject. It is my hope that in the next few years we shall be able to present more detailed and incisive analyses of some of the issues discussed in this book.

During the latter part of 1971, all of 1972, and the first part of 1973, I was a member of the President's Advisory Panel on Timber and the Environment; its report was published in 1973 by the U.S. Government Printing Office. To some degree, my thinking has matured since the Panel report was published, but the present book is in no sense a repudiation or a contradiction of the Panel report. I not only signed the latter, as one member of the Panel, but I fully endorse its findings. This book draws heavily on the facts and analyses of the Panel report, yet it is not simply a summary or a restatement of the Panel report. Hopefully, as an individual I can present the forest policy issues more sharply—perhaps more starkly—than could a committee or than would be proper in a governmental document. The Panel report presents recommendations to the President in which I concurred fully; the present book states conclusions but does not present recommendations. Admittedly, the difference between conclusions and recommendations is partly semantic, but I think it is also real. The discerning reader will detect differences in approach and exposition between the Panel report and this book, but they are complementary to a considerable degree.

I must acknowledge my great debt to my fellow panel members (the late Fred A. Seaton, Ralph D. Hodges, Jr., Stephen A. Spurr, and Donald J. Zinn), and to the Panel staff (particularly Henry Van Zile Hyde, Jr., Hardy L. Shirley, William Jolly, and Susan Whisnant) and to the Panel's numerous consultants. They stimulated my interest, they provided me with facts and ideas, and—above all—forced me to think more carefully than I had ever done before about some of the subjects treated herein. It was a most stimulating and valuable experience for me to have served on the Panel. At the same time, of course, I must absolve them of responsibility for what I say herein, for that is mine alone.

In May 1974, Resources for the Future conducted a forum on forest policy. The papers presented at this forum and a summary of the discussions have been published by RFF.[1] At the forum nearly 200 persons, informed and concerned about forests, with widely varying professional and interest group backgrounds, entered into the discussion. This forum was enormously helpful to me, and I am glad to acknowledge my debt to those who participated in it.

In this book I have relied heavily upon data collected and published by the U.S. Forest Service. My interpretation of the data sometimes differs from that of the Forest Service, and I sometimes comment upon the inadequacies of the data, but I have no resources to collect new and original data which would in any way extend, confirm, or repudiate the Forest Service data. Like every other writer on forestry matters, I am deeply in the debt of the Forest Service for the data it has been able to assemble.

My professional training is in economics, and this naturally affects my viewpoint and the way I approach issues of policy. I am not a forester nor have I had training in forestry; neither am I an ecologist, a wild life expert, nor any one of several other related professionals. Naturally, as one who has dealt with natural resource matters for many years, I have picked up some understanding and some knowledge about these various fields. The forests of the United States, including the national forests, have great value, and their best management is an economic problem—as well as a problem in

---

[1] Forest Policy for the Future, RFF Working Paper LW-1 (Washington: Resources for the Future, Inc., 1974).

silviculture, ecology, public administration, and various other fields of human knowledge. I have tried in this book to avoid the technical jargon of economists, as far as possible. More importantly, I propose a framework of analysis for forest policy which goes well beyond economics as the latter is ordinarily defined.

In order to avoid unnecessary errors, I have had several of my friends and professional colleagues read an earlier draft of this manuscript, and it surely is more accurate and clearer as a result of their comments. I am indebted to my colleague, William F. Hyde, for help in compiling and checking some of the data, to Charlene Semer and Joan Tron for editorial assistance, and to Diantha Stevenson and Jean Edes for secretarial assistance.

MARION CLAWSON
Washington
August 1974

# FORESTS
# FOR WHOM
# AND FOR
# WHAT?

# 1.

## Why Concern
## Ourselves with
## Forest Policy?

Forests serve the American people in many ways and have the potential to serve more people in better and more generous ways. Everyone uses wood in some form—in such simple household uses as facial tissue, toilet paper, newspapers, and wrapping materials; as paper in various forms in offices and stores; as furniture; and as an essential component of all new construction for homes, offices, factories, and stores. Indeed, it is difficult to conceive of anyone who does not use wood in some form. He would have to live in a cave, use stone furniture, burn coal picked off the surface of the land, and have found some nonwood substitute for toilet paper. Much of the water used in homes, in factories, for miscellaneous urban purposes, and for irrigation flows from watersheds that are largely or wholly forested. At least half, and perhaps considerably more, of the total population engages in outdoor recreation on both public and privately owned land, much of which is forested, and forests, particularly their edges where they meet open land, are the home for a rich and varied wildlife. In all these ways, and others that are less obvious or affect smaller numbers of people, forests of one kind or another affect all people—some, of course, more than others, and in different ways, but no one in the United States today is wholly independent of forests.

The importance of forests in the total natural resource scene can be measured in several ways. Forests are a major land use; they occupy 33 percent of the total land area of the country—754 million acres today in all fifty states. Two-thirds of this, 500 million acres, is occupied by "commercial" forests and the remainder by forests reserved from harvest, such as those in national parks and those of too low productivity for economic wood production.[1] Only the grazing

[1] Some activities use forest (and other) land but not the forest (trees); for instance, roads, transmission lines, mining, grazing, and even second home development where the use of trees is similar to that on suburban lots. These land uses are not considered in this book.

1

of domestic livestock on nonforested natural range lands uses about as much land in the United States as does forests; all other kinds of land use are concentrated on much smaller areas. It must be pointed out that the very much smaller area of land used for residential, commercial, and other urban purposes has a much higher value (not including buildings and other improvements) than does forest land. But forests are major land occupiers by whatever precise measure one cares to use.

Forests are important in many other ways as well. Approximately 70,000 persons are employed directly in forests and another million or more in forest processing industries. About 5 percent of the gross national product arises from the use of forest products, which, in economic planning and management have assumed an unusual importance in the past half dozen or so years. Prices of forest products have fluctuated widely because of a high level of housing production, stimulated in part by government programs; because of a high level of export demand for logs and other forest products; and because of restrictions in timber supply, in part resulting from stricter environmental protection measures. Twice since 1968 the price of stumpage (the standing tree in the forest), the price of harvested logs, and the price of finished and semifinished products, such as lumber, have mounted rapidly to levels previously unknown and then have quickly receded, at least part way, to former levels. Lumber and other wood products contribute 2.65 percent to the weighting in the general wholesale price index. When lumber prices have doubled in a year, as they have twice in recent inflationary periods, the direct effect is to pull the whole price index upward by 2.65 percent; the secondary effect may be equally great, as other prices are adjusted to a higher level and as wages are readjusted by a cost-of-living formula. Thus, unusual attention has focused on price movements of lumber and other forest products, especially in periods of rapidly rising prices—when lumber prices fall, the public seems to pay much less attention.

The services and products provided by the forests not only have value and importance to the American public, but it would not be easy to find substitute sources of services or materials if forest areas or supplies were somehow cut off or reduced. Outdoor recreation is possible in many situations other than forests, yet a forest—or at least a number of trees—is a highly valuable asset for any outdoor recreation area. Forests are often a valuable feature of the wilderness scene. Many watersheds are not forested, yet forests cover much of the more valuable watershed areas of the country. Other building materials exist which in some circumstances can be economically used, but wood has the great advantage of being renewable—it grows rather than being exhaustible as is iron ore, bauxite, or other aluminum sources, and the various fuels needed to process the metals.[2] Transformation of wood from standing tree to final construction material requires vastly less energy than does the comparable transformation of ore to construction metal or of limestone to cement. As a result, the environmental impact of producing wood is generally far less than the environmental impact of producing any substitute building material. In addition, wood is biodegradable in a way that metals are not. Wood can be disposed of more easily and more quickly than other building materials when it is no longer usable in its original or primary purpose. As the nation becomes more conservation-minded, the potentialities of wood loom larger.

FOREST POLICY HAS LONG BEEN A
NATIONAL CONCERN

The United States has long had national programs of one kind or another concerned with forests. The establishment of the "forest reserves"—now called national forests—began in 1891. Their administration has been the subject of much legislation and debate in the intervening years, and continues so today. There is a substantial cooperative program of fire prevention and control for forests of all ownerships, financed in part by the federal government and in large part by the states and private landowners. A similar program is available for insect and disease control. There are also research programs on various aspects of forestry; these are largely federal, but some are also sponsored by other levels of government. There are extensive programs of direct aid to private forest owners—technical assistance, seedlings for planting, and the like. There have been limitations on exports of logs harvested from federal lands, and there have been proposals to limit total wood export. All of these and other public programs affect forests and forest owners directly.

In addition, there are many public programs which indirectly affect forestry to a significant extent. Transportation, taxation, housing, foreign trade, monetary, and other public programs have often had a major effect on forest output and on utilization of forest goods and services. Educational and research programs have also had substantial, though indirect, effect.

[2] For a somewhat detailed discussion of this subject, with quantitative data and with sources, see Jerome Saeman, "Solving Resource and Environmental Problems by the More Efficient Utilization of Timber," *Report of the President's Advisory Panel on Timber and the Environment*, Appendix K (Washington: Government Printing Office, 1973).

CONTROVERSIES OVER FOREST POLICY

The past decade or so has seen the initiation or the expansion of several controversies about forests in the United States. These controversies have been more concerned with public than with privately owned forests, yet the latter have not escaped entirely. Some of the controversy has found expression in attempts to obtain or to prevent legislation, especially federal legislation. As such, it often takes place in Congressional committee hearings or through efforts to influence individual Congressmen. But some of the controversy has taken place within or been directed toward the Executive Branch—the effort to get or to oppose an Executive Order, for instance. These are traditional ways of trying to influence governmental action for the benefit of some interest group, usually at the expense of other groups or of the general public; they are not limited to forestry matters, or to natural resource issues, but extend to all governmental activities.

A new feature in the formulation of public policy—in practice, operative largely for various natural resource issues—has been the use of the court suit, especially one brought by groups of interested citizens. The building of a road into a roadless area is stopped by injunction of a court of appropriate jurisdiction, or a timber sale is stopped in the same way, or the construction of a pipeline to carry oil across public lands is similarly opposed. The National Environmental Policy Act of 1970 not only expressed national concern over the environment, but its requirement for environmental impact statements for "major" federal projects or actions required federal agencies to direct more attention to environmental problems than they had done in the past, and at the same time gave the citizen interest groups a more convenient procedure for opposing actions with which they disagreed. Many of the suits have charged that the federal agency involved did not adequately comply with this provision of the Act.

At the same time, the courts of the nation have been both taking a greater interest in environmental matters and relaxing the conditions under which citizen groups may sue. At an earlier date, intervention in the courts was limited to those who could show a direct, personal, economic interest in the proposed public action. Today, "standing to sue" has been greatly widened—just how much, perhaps only future court actions will define precisely. The balance of power between the "conservationist" citizen group and industry has shifted dramatically and suddenly toward the former, at least for the present. Only a hardy prophet would deny the possibility of some future reverse shift in power.

Many thoughtful observers of natural resource use and management doubt that adversary proceedings before a court are the most efficient way to formulate national or social policy. Such proceedings often ignore or neglect the interests of groups that are not parties to the legal controversy. The courts and the antagonists often are unable to explore possible solutions, such as new management programs, new investments and the like, which might give each party to the controversy a large part, but perhaps not all, of what each sought. The gains by one party need not be exactly and precisely at the expense of other parties; there may be better solutions than this.

The forest policy issues discussed in this book are believed to be particularly timely for the 1973 to 1975 period, but they did not arise in these years for the first time; many of them have been around for a relatively long time. Nor are they likely all to be ended soon—some are hardy perennials. Some of the specific issues will require the attention of the Ford Administration and will be fought before the 93rd and 94th Congresses; but some will engage the attention of the President elected in 1976, whoever he may be and from whichever party he may come, and of the 95th and 96th and sucessive Congresses. Most forest policy issues have not been partisan political party issues; more typically, there have been diverse interests within each party. On many of the issues, a Congressman will be subjected to divergent interests and pressures from within his district. Still further, many of the issues are not exclusively issues for public action; private actions and decisions may be highly important for some.

# 2.

## Pressing Issues of Forest Policy

Among the many policy issues involving forests, perhaps half a dozen may fairly be described as "major" or "pressing" in the sense that they currently engage the attention and the efforts of considerable numbers of people on a national scale. These are briefly described in this chapter; in Chapter 12, after our presentation of facts and analyses, we come back to these policy issues again.

Every policy issue in every field is controversial; if there were no major differences of opinion, there would be no issue. Different persons and different groups have different interests. The basic problem of a society and its government is to resolve policy issues by finding ways which most nearly reconcile the numerous and contending interests. It is absurd to suggest that solutions which give every interest essentially all its wants can always be found, or that any "solution" benefits every party to the controversy; some persons and interests inevitably gain while others lose, or some gain more than do others. Good social policy includes identification of gainers and losers, with as close an estimate as possible of the magnitudes of the gains and losses, and with a final decision which at least considers all major interests. It is also absurd to suggest that every party at interest has equal weight or influence in the final decision; some persons and some interests are, always have been, and likely always will be more influential than others. The democratic ethic and the belief in equal rights for all persons cannot wholly negate variations in ability, in economic and political power, and in economic stake in the outcome. Good social policy, in a democratic society, includes recognition of the rights of all concerned parties, but it does not preclude giving greater weight to some interests than to others.

Merely to define or state policy issues is difficult. There are clearly several issues, each somewhat distinct and separate yet closely related to others. Decisions on one issue may greatly affect positions on other issues; alliances and opponents on one issue may to some extent be similarly lined up on another issue and yet often somewhat differently aligned also. The discussion that follows is not neatly logical; some issues overlap or intertwine with others. Nevertheless, it seems useful to outline several more or less identifiable forest policy issues which concern significant numbers of people in the United States.

## HOW MUCH LAND TO DEVOTE TO FORESTS

One policy issue is how much land to use for forests in the United States; the issue of what to use the forests for will be discussed later. At present, one-third of the nation's land area is in forests of some kind, and nearly one-fourth is in "commercial" forests. Are these acreages too large or too small? This question in turn breaks down into two parts: How much effort, if any, should be directed toward retaining presently forested areas in forest uses? And what efforts, if any, should be directed toward restoring or developing forest cover on land capable of forest tree growth but now lacking any trees or lacking a reasonably satisfactory stand of trees?

Some land uses in the United States are expanding almost inevitably as a consequence of population growth and increasing per capita incomes. Included here is land for residential and other urban uses, for highways and other transportation uses, for reservoirs to provide water supply, and other uses. As these uses have expanded, they have encroached upon cropland and forest land, as well as upon other land uses and land types. Concern has been expressed in some quarters about the conversion of the best-grade croplands to various urban uses. In spite of much talk, no effective action has yet been taken to limit such land conversions, nor does it seem probable that any effective action will be taken in the future—landowners are too eager to reap the gains from rising land values, for one thing.

Some forest land has been "lost" to these same land conversions. In addition, some forested land has been cleared for cropping. In earlier decades this took a great deal of land out of forestry, but in more recent decades such conversions have been on a limited scale. Partially offsetting the loss of forest land to other uses has been some reversion of abandoned cropland to forests. There has been relatively less public and professional concern over maintenance of good forest land in forests than there has been of retention of good cropland in crops. Such concern as there has been has more generally been about unusual stands of trees than about forests in general. Nevertheless, the issue of protecting forest land for continued forestry has existed and might become more serious in the future.

A policy issue of more practical importance relates to the restoration of forests on sites where the former stand has been destroyed by fire or by cutting, and on abandoned croplands where no trees or a wholly inadequate stand has developed from natural seeding. Forest Service data suggest that 21 million acres of productive forest land, 3⅓ million acres of which are within national forests, are non-stocked; in addition, other areas are understocked. The costs of satisfactorily restocking this land would be considerable—of the general magnitude of $62 million for national forests alone. Substantial replanting has taken place on both private and public forests, but the problem of restocking remains. In many cases, economic analysis will show a modest yet reasonable return from restocking.

The policy issues on restocking former forest sites revolve around a number of questions. Is this the best use to make of private or public funds available for investment in forests? Could a greater output of wood be secured more economically by using the same funds to practice more intensive forestry on lands now in forest? Could the other outputs of forests be achieved more economically in some other way? What species should be replanted, if replanting is undertaken? For what should the replanted forests be used? Who should bear the costs, and who is likely to get the benefits from public programs of forest planting? What are the nontimber benefits of reforestation?

## HOW MUCH FOREST LAND TO WITHDRAW FROM HARVEST

A policy issue of vastly more popular appeal, but logically subordinate, is how much forest land to withdraw from harvest either temporarily or permanently. Withdrawals may be for national or state parks, to preserve scenic values, for wilderness uses, for various conservation purposes, or for other uses. In each case, by the value standards of the withdrawal proponents, the value of the "natural," or undisturbed, or existing forest is greater than the values that could be created by timber harvest. In many cases, proponents of withdrawal have not stated their case in economic terms and would reject a formal economic analysis; instead, they stress other values.

This type of policy issue arises when proposals are made to establish national or state parks containing significant volumes of standing timber or significant capacity to produce wood. It arose in the 1930s over the establishment of Olympic National Park. In more recent times, it has arisen over the boundaries of the North Cascades

National Park, the Redwood National Park, and land withdrawals in Alaska, among others.

Parts of national forests had been withdrawn by executive action from many uses, including timber harvest, for wilderness areas in the years prior to 1964. In that year, Congress passed the National Wilderness Reservation Act, giving legislative protection to wilderness areas established under the Act. Some areas of national forests, national parks, and federal wildlife areas have been withdrawn as wilderness under this Act. By 1973, vociferous claims for large-scale additional withdrawals were being made. In national forests, some 1,440 roadless areas, each of 5,000 acres or more in extent, were identified as candidates for wilderness consideration. Additional areas were under consideration in national parks, wildlife refuges, and other federal lands.

Numerous questions of fact, of social objectives, and of policy arise out of any proposal for withdrawal. How much standing timber exists on the roadless areas? How much of this land is capable of sustained forestry? What would be its annual timber output? How suitable are these areas for wilderness use? More specifically, how strict a definition of "wilderness" should be applied? For example, is mere roadlessness enough? How much human modification of the landscape is permissible? If withdrawn or established as wilderness, how much use can any area withstand and yet retain its wilderness character? Who would be the beneficiaries of wilderness withdrawals and who would bear the costs (including loss of income from other uses foregone)? Similarly, if timber harvest is permitted, or if intensive recreation facilities are developed and thus the wilderness is denied, who benefits and who pays costs? How can wilderness values be identified and measured? Are we content to accept an approximation of the economic values of wilderness experiences as the measure of value, or do we include other types of value?

A generally parallel set of considerations and issues arises for the aesthetic or scenic values of forests. Many people like to view a forest, either close at hand as they drive through it, or on a distant hillside, or as they walk along paths through forests. In addition to all these questions about the costs, benefits, and beneficiaries of wilderness areas, a further question can be raised about scenic values: Will the forest prized today for its appearance still look essentially the same a decade or several decades from now? In particular, may wind, insects, or other natural forces materially modify if not destroy the present forest? If the present forest cannot persist unchanged, might it be better to utilize wood from the trees that would otherwise be lost? Or is the natural sequence of change a basic reason to preserve a wilderness unmodified by man? Sometimes, or for some people, managed forests are both more attractive and more readily usable by the public than are fully mature natural forests.

## HOW TO HARVEST TIMBER

Another forest policy issue which has aroused much popular interest relates to methods of timber harvest and, more particularly, to the practice of clearcutting timber stands. The arguments advanced by proponents to support clearcutting are: it is the best way, or perhaps the only way, to get satisfactory regeneration of a new stand for species which will not grow in heavy shade; even for species which will grow in mixed age stands, clearcutting may be necessary to remove undesirable trees in order to establish a new and better forest by complete restocking; restocking with genetically superior strains and species of trees is possible only on clearcut areas; control of some diseases, such as dwarf mistletoe, is possible only when all mature trees have been cut; environmental impacts of timber harvest are less when roads are used only once and then closed out, than when they are kept open for continuous harvest on a selection cut basis; and clearcutting is often far and away the most economical method of harvesting.

All of these claims are rejected or denied by the opponents of clearcutting. Their most effective arguments have been photographs of newly clearcut areas, many of which look like heavily scarred battlefields. Many such photographs have appeared in newspapers and popular outlets, with devastating effect—they bring the clearcutting issue down to a human scale, to considerations easily grasped by the most casual reader or observer. Many old growth stands contain much rotten or partially rotten wood, which it does not pay to remove from the forest; clearcutting reveals the volume of such wood starkly. The fact that selective cutting of the same stands might have left as much rotten wood in the forest, but largely concealed by the remaining trees, is ignored. Proponents of clearcutting have repeatedly charged its opponents with ignoring or neglecting the many successful regenerations of new and thriftier forests while emphasizing the instances of failure to secure regeneration. On the propaganda front, the opponents of clearcutting have generally won.

The clearcutting issue on national forests was at least partially resolved by a Senate committee report.[1] This report stated:

Clear-cutting should not be used as a cutting method on Federal land areas where:
a. Soil, slope or other watershed conditions are fragile and subject to major injury.
b. There is no assurance that the area can be adequately restocked within five years after harvest.
c. Aesthetic values outweigh other considerations.
d. The method is preferred only because it will give the greatest dollar return or the greatest unit output.
*Clear-cutting should be used only where:*
a. It is determined to be silviculturally essential to accomplish the relevant forest management objectives.
b. The size of clear-cut blocks, patches or strips are kept at the minimum necessary to accomplish silvicultural and other multiple-use forest management objectives.
c. A multidisciplinary review has first been made of the potential environmental, biological, aesthetic, engineering and economic impacts on each sale area.
d. Clear-cut blocks, patches or strips are, in all cases, shaped and blended as much as possible with the natural terrain.

While this report was accepted by the Forest Service and other federal agencies as a basis for timber harvest, the clearcutting issue was not finally settled in this way. Opponents have continued to press for firmer and more restrictive controls, and in late 1973 a bill was introduced in Congress to control clearcutting on national forests. On a more general level, the clearcutting controversy is evidence of a significant popular interest in forestry practices—a matter which until a comparatively few years ago seemed to be the province of foresters. Many foresters still hold an elitist view of such matters: only one with professional training can express a reasonable judgment on such technical forestry issues.

A nonforester and an outsider, such as the present author, cannot help but wonder how far the clearcutting controversy was efficient. As in many an emotional issue, there is grave doubt that the right questions are being asked and debated, let alone that the right answers are being made. Admitting that clearcutting produces aesthe-

[1] U.S. Senate Committee on Interior and Insular Affairs, Subcommittee on Public Lands, *Clearcutting on Federal Timberlands*, 92nd Cong., 2nd sess. (Washington: U.S. Government Printing Office, March 1972), p. 9.

tically and environmentally distressing results—at least temporarily —in many if not all cases, would some other method of timber harvest actually have been better in the long-run history of the forest? Was the issue really clearcutting, or cutting by any means? Should some of the areas clearcut have been reserved uncut for other uses?

NATIONAL FOREST MANAGEMENT

Many aspects of national forest administration have been the subject of controversy—indeed, many of the other issues described in this chapter relate in part to national forests and thus could be considered issues of national forest administration. In this section, our concern is with only one aspect of national forest management: how fast to liquidate, or indeed how far ever to liquidate, the mature old growth timber stands which typify many western national forests.

The specific facts about these forests will be sketched briefly in later chapters. On the simplest level, these old growth forests contain an immense volume of standing timber—close to half the volume of standing softwood sawtimber in the nation; they are growing slowly or not at all, with rot, windthrow, disease, and fire often taking as much wood annually as is grown; those stands not reserved from cutting are being cut on a schedule which will result in their liquidation over a 100-year period, more or less.

How much of such forests should be reserved for aesthetic or other reasons? How long could they in fact be reserved, given the natural hazards to such timber stands? Should their rate of harvest be accelerated to yield a greater output of timber from national forests for the next decade or two and to put these forests in condition for growing more wood annually? What happens to national forest timber output when the old growth stands have been liquidated? Can the growth of new young forests provide an equal continuing supply of timber?

This policy issue, or this set of policy issues, has aroused nothing like the popular concern that the clearcutting issue has provoked. These issues are not so easily simplified and dramatized for the nonspecialist. When proposals for accelerating harvest of mature old growth timber on national forests have been raised, a conventional answer has been to assert the virtues of sustained yield, but this is far from being as simple and unequivocal an answer as it is often pictured. In addition, the *economic* aspects of this policy issue are extremely important.

OUTPUT FROM SMALL PRIVATE FORESTS

Approximately 60 percent of the nation's forest area is in "other" ownerships, meaning that it is privately (not publicly) owned and is owned by persons or corporations who are not also timber processors. Much of this land is in ownerships too small to be operated economically as single forest enterprises. Many of the small privately owned forests are owned for reasons other than profit from growing wood—for their recreational value, for hope of speculative profit from a rise in land values, because the land was inherited and there is some sentimental attachment to it, and for other similar reasons.

Almost every study of forests in a region or area shows that the small private forests are managed less intensively than are the larger private forests or than are the public forests in the same region or area. Some land will be unstocked, much more will have stands of trees incapable of producing as much wood as the soil and climate are capable of producing, species composition of stands may be poor, and other deficiencies will be apparent. Such small forests are typically harvested at irregular intervals, more because the owner seeks income than for silvicultural reasons. Harvests often leave the forest in poor productive condition; in particular, many trees of barely merchantable size, that would grow relatively rapidly if left, are taken. Small owners often realize far less than the full value of their timber when they do make a sale.

Several public programs to aid small private forest owners have been undertaken in the past. Fire control, either free or at charges far less than full cost, has benefited many small forest owners who could not possibly have maintained their own fire fighting organization. Likewise, insect and disease control programs which have aided small private forest owners have been maintained at public expense. Various direct subsidy programs, such as provision of planting stock, have also aided them. In addition, various forms of educational or technical assistance have been directed toward the small forest owners. The results of many of these various public programs have been disappointingly unproductive.

Several policy issues arise out of this general situation. Is there a public interest in increasing the output of small private forests that is sufficient to warrant the expenditure of public funds for this purpose? If so, what is the optimum level of public support? If past programs have been less successful than is desirable, are there new kinds of programs or new approaches which just might be more successful? All these issues will be explored more fully in later chapters. The large total acreage of small private forests and their large unrealized production potential makes them of much more importance than they would be if they represented a smaller proportion of the national forest area.

## TIMBER NEEDS AND ENVIRONMENTAL CONSTRAINTS

Wood is an essential raw material. As the population of the United States increases and as per capita incomes rise, the demand for wood, or for some substitute for wood in its present uses, will surely rise. Residential construction, for instance, has been very high, by historical standards, since about 1968 and promises to continue to be high for many years ahead. Residential construction is a function of the number of new households formed annually more than it is of the total number of people in the population. Children born in the "baby boom" of the postwar years are now reaching adulthood and requiring living quarters of their own. Many thousands of relatively affluent people are building or buying vacation or other second homes. To these construction uses of wood must be added increasing demands for wood use in paper and other products.

At the same time, demands for the forests for other uses, such as recreation and wilderness, are also rising, as is the popular concern over the "environment" and the aesthetic appearance of the forests. This concern underlies the issues of how much forest to withdraw from harvest and how to harvest the forests which are cut. But some environmental concern goes beyond those issues or takes different forms. What happens to the quality of stream flow when forests are harvested? Does timber harvest unduly drain soil fertility and in time seriously reduce the capacity of the land to grow trees? Does timber harvest adversely affect wildlife in the forests? Will timber harvest methods result in unacceptable soil erosion? How much value should be attached to the aesthetics of the forests, how may these be preserved during timber harvest, and who is prepared to bear the costs of aesthetic preservation?

These are rather general concerns, not as specific or as easily dramatized as the wilderness and clearcutting issues, but perhaps they are of greater importance because they are more generalized. As with the other policy issues set forth in this chapter, the purpose here is merely to raise the issue, leaving a fuller discussion of it for later.

## EXPORT OF FOREST PRODUCTS

Another issue which has raised a good deal of popular interest involves the export of timber products from the United States, and more specifically the export of logs (or squared-up logs called cants) from the Pacific Northwest to Japan. The foreign trade of the United States in forest products is briefly this: we import a lot of lumber from western Canada and a lot of paper or pulpwood from eastern Canada; we import some hardwoods, or hardwood veneers and plywood, from south Asian sources; we export some paper to western Europe; and we export logs and cants, wood chips, and some other products to Japan. There are other smaller trade flows, but these include the major ones. The reasons behind these flows are numerous and sometimes complex. In general, wood products are heavy, bulky, and relatively low-valued for their weight, hence long-distance movement by land is usually uneconomic. Shipment by water may be more economic, but the United States prohibits freight movements between U.S. ports except in U.S. owned and operated vessels. Because U.S. water freight rates are very high, this prohibition effectively precludes movement of nearly all Alaskan wood products to other states but makes their export to Japan economic, and it favors Canadian lumber shipments to the East Coast over U.S. shipments.

In recent years, Japan has been buying wood where it could find it. Japan has been increasing its economic output at a phenomenal rate, with a rising affluence on the part of substantial sectors of its population. At the same time, the standard of housing in Japan is unbelievably low by western standards. A program of housing construction as large in total as that for the United States and twice as large in proportion to the respective populations has been undertaken by the Japanese government in recent years. Such a program requires a great deal of wood. In addition, the rising economic output requires more wood for paper, both for industry and for households.

Japan is forested, but the actual acreage of forests is limited because these islands are relatively small. Although its timber output could be increased, the country must reach out for needed wood supplies. It has sought wood in eastern Siberia, along the coast of North and South America, and elsewhere. The Japanese have much preferred to buy logs (or cants) and resaw them to their own specifications, which are different from our lumber sizes and quality grades. At the same time, British Columbia has prohibited the export of unsawn logs from Province-owned forests (which includes nearly all of the forest land in the Province), although it is eager to export lumber to the United States and elsewhere.

In the fall of 1972 Japanese log buyers engaged in a most un-Japaneselike degree of competition with one another, which pushed log prices to unheard-of levels. Negotiations with the Japanese government seem to have led to some restraint in their purchases in the United States; and with the decline in lumber and plywood prices which took place in 1973, some of the heat for the limitation of log exports.to Japan has evaporated. But the issue of exporting raw materials and more specifically of exporting wood in one of its many forms is far from dead, nor is it likely to be so in the future. The pros and cons of government action to limit these exports are outlined in chapter 7. It is ironic that the United States, a long-term importer of raw materials, should consider limiting the export of *its* raw materials now, when competition has pushed price levels up.

The issues enumerated here do not include all of the issues of forest policy that face the United States today, but they include the "major" issues—at least by this author's definition. In no case has the issue been fully stated, much less fully explored, nor have alternative solutions been suggested. That is the task for the following chapters.

# 3.

## A Framework of
## Analysis for
## Forest Policy

An intelligent and efficient consideration of forest policy requires a framework of analysis to organize the discussion so that the differing views of the various parties may be contrasted. A large part of the distressingly high quotient of heat and of the distressingly low quotient of light generated in most discussions of policy arises from the lack of a systematic way of organizing facts, opinions, and policy positions. If all the parties to a policy dispute could agree upon a framework of analysis, that would be wonderful; if at least some parties have their own framework of analysis, that is better than nothing; but if no one has a considered plan of analysis, the result is likely to be confusion confounded—a stimulating show perhaps but unlikely to reach a consistent conclusion.

The purpose of this chapter is to set forth a scheme of analysis for consideration of forest policy. An attempt has been made to develop a comprehensive and eclectic framework for policy analysis. It is not limited to economic considerations, nor to ecological or silvicultural ones, nor to sociological factors, but combines these and others. There are serious disadvantages to such a comprehensive framework, which will be considered at the end of this chapter. But there are greater weaknesses in a narrower scheme of analysis which utilizes fewer kinds of information, employs a simpler analytical technique, and is almost certain to produce "answers" that some— perhaps most—parties to a policy dispute will find unacceptable.

The scheme of analysis for policy discussions on forestry set forth in this chapter includes five parts: physical and biological feasibility and consequences, economic efficiency, economic equity, social or cultural acceptability, and operational or administrative practicality. While there is, in this author's mind, some logic in the sequence of these five parts, there is no suggestion of ranking by importance —each is equally important, even equally critical.

## PHYSICAL AND BIOLOGICAL FEASIBILITY
## AND CONSEQUENCES

There is no real sense in talking about a forest policy that is not physically and biologically feasible—redwoods will not grow on the Mohave Desert, nor can areas above timberline be forested, to use two extreme examples. But practical issues of physical feasibility are implicit in some of the policy issues sketched in chapter 2. Must Douglas fir be clearcut in order to establish new stands of the same species? Is the answer the same for moister northern slopes as for warmer and drier southern slopes? Is it the same for areas in the northern and cooler parts of the range of this species as for the warmer and drier southern and eastern edges of its range? Is the only way to grow lodgepole pine on a site now covered with a mature stand which is heavily infested with dwarf mistletoe to clearcut all the present stand and expect a natural reseeding from surrounding uncut areas? If such a stand is not now cut, and the timber salvaged, will it all blow down in a storm within a few years or be killed by some disease or insect attack, or may it stand for decades? What are the physical and biological alternatives? If trees are harvested, whether by clearcutting or by selective cutting, what effect will this have upon each kind of wildlife which is now present on the site or may invade it after cutting? Which species are harmed by timber harvest, and which are benefited? How long do harmful and beneficial effects last?

These are but illustrative of the kinds of questions about physical and biological feasibility and consequences that will be raised in every important forest policy issue. One can be fairly sure that there will be major differences of opinion as to the "facts" in nearly all policy controversies. The silviculturalist is likely to take one position on the cutting of the lodgepole pine stand, in the example cited above, while the preservationist is likely to take a different position —each basing his view upon his understanding of the facts. There are several reasons for the divergences of opinion about the physical facts of a forest situation: forests are enormously variable, and what is true of one forest may not be true of another which is nevertheless similar in many other respects; many forest situations have not been studied fully, primarily due to lack of funds, but sometimes because the need for certain information was not clear until a policy issue had already risen; the relevant facts often concern a future response to a present action, and this is particularly difficult to predict.

The social scientist or the policy maker should expect to find the facts as to physical and biological relationships in dispute in any policy controversy. A decision must nearly always be reached, and a line of action taken when there is some doubt—perhaps serious doubt—as to its factual basis. It is easy to suggest postponing the decision until all the relevant facts are in hand. But sometimes the relevant facts will never be in hand until some line of action has been carried out, and sometimes decisions simply cannot wait. In the example of harvesting the mistletoe-infested mature lodgepole pine stand, it may be impossible to be certain what the effect of harvesting will be until it is actually carried out; to postpone the decision may be to let the weather make it—by blowing down the present stand.

There is a further corollary of this lack of assurance about the physical facts: there is an element of risk or chance in every decision. A stand of some kind of trees may be harvested, by any method, with certain expectations as to the kind, rate, and adequacy of the subsequent natural regeneration. Favorable weather, or even average weather, may indeed produce the expected results, but unfavorable weather may negate them. What then? What means exist for remedying an undesired result? Is the decision maker prepared to accept the economic and social consequences of a certain percentage of failures? Can the public be taught to realize that variation in biological results is inevitable, and that some failures of reasoned programs are to be expected?

Early in any debate over forest policy, it is helpful to outline the relevant issues of physical and biological feasibility and physical and biological consequences, to get as much agreement about the actual facts as the disputants are prepared to accept, and, if possible, to isolate and set bounds to the range within which the probable answers to disputed facts fall. All this may be very difficult, yet it is basic; without it, all further policy debate is likely to be dubious or sterile.

ECONOMIC EFFICIENCY

As questions of physical and biological feasibility and physical and biological consequences narrow down from "whether" to "how much," considerations of economic efficiency begin to arise. What are the costs and what are the gains from a particular proposed line of action? How much capital will be required, what is a reasonable interest rate, when will the capital be returned, what are the risks of failure, how liquid or illiquid is the investment, and so forth? How much labor, of what skills, and at what cost, will be required? And so on, for all items of cost. On the other side of the ledger, what are the probable returns in monetary terms? When will they accrue? How vulnerable is the enterprise to the vagaries of markets? How far is a particular proposed line of forest management dependent upon the historical upward trend in lumber and stumpage prices?

Particularly troublesome are the numerous outputs of the forest or activities in the forest which are not customarily sold in the market place. These include intensive outdoor recreation, wilderness experiences, wildlife values, watershed values, aesthetic values, and perhaps others. Most people will agree that these outputs of the typical forest possess value, but great differences of opinion arise as to the relative amounts of such values. Some approaches to evaluating these forest outputs have been made in recent years, and more can be done, yet a large measure of intangibility will always surround many of these values.

Economic analysis of the value of forest outputs is to some degree independent of the realization of these benefits in cash terms; that is, one may estimate the value of the recreation opportunity, even when no one pays for this opportunity. There is a social value created, which can be estimated even when there is no cash or market counterpart. But the cautious economist or administrator is wary of these value estimates when no one pays for the services provided because there is a sturdily built-in incentive to exaggerate the amount of the benefit. For instance, beneficiaries have not been required to pay for the benefits gained from the flood protection and navigation improvement programs of the United States, and the tendency to exaggerate benefits has run unrestrained; had some person or group been required to pay for the benefits gained, claims of benefits might have shrunk dramatically. The doctor who treats midnight gastric pains is hailed as a life saver, but when his bill for a house call comes at the end of the month, the patient admits only a slight stomachache.

Economic analysis can show the efficiency of producing one forest output as compared with another or one mixture of outputs as compared with another mixture; of utilizing one production and management technique as compared with another; of investing varying amounts of capital, labor, and management skills; and of other aspects of forest policy. Should the relatively unproductive sites within national forests be harvested, or might it be better to concentrate available funds on more intensive management of the more productive sites? In all such analyses, the economist is completely dependent upon the silviculturalist, the engineer, the wildlife biologist, and other physical or biological specialists to tell him the physical and biological costs and results of alternative lines of management. Without this information, he cannot make the appropriate economic analysis.

Sophisticated methods of economic analysis of costs and benefits from natural resource management and development have been developed in recent decades. These are powerful and useful tools, but they suffer at least two basic weaknesses: first, they are no stronger than the factual base upon which they rest, and they embody certain assumptions as to the nature of the society—income distribution, for example—which may be challenged; and secondly, they take no account of the incidence of the benefits created and of the costs incurred. Who gains, and who pays? It is to these latter questions that we now turn.

ECONOMIC WELFARE OR EQUITY

The economic benefits of some program of forest management accrue to certain individuals or groups, and the costs fall on certain individuals or groups. Only rarely, if ever, will the two groups be identical in composition and will the proportion of benefits and costs be exactly equal. If a productive forest area is set aside for wilderness use or for intensive recreation, the persons who use it and the businesses which supply them, benefit; if it is a national forest, the loss of income from timber production decreases revenues to the Treasury as well as employment opportunities in harvesting and processing the wood; if lumber and other forest product prices increase, houses are more costly, and much of the real burden falls on urban people living far from the forest site. Many more examples of divergences of benefits and costs could be cited.

Subject to the uncertainties and possible inaccuracies of basic data, economic calculations can often answer the question of which method of forest management produces the greater net economic benefits; they can at least show how large the costs are even though benefits may be intangible and immeasurable. But economic efficiency calculations alone do not show the incidence of benefits and of costs; that requires additional analysis. Moreover, economic efficiency is cold comfort to the person or group that loses out or gains less than it sought.

It is often possible to identify the groups or even the individuals who gain by various forest management programs and to estimate the amount of such gain or loss. For economic efficiency, there is (at least superficially) a quantitative measure of net gain, and one program which maximizes net benefits. There is no corresponding neat measure of economic welfare or equity results and no apparently unequivocal measure of "better." That is, by skillful and diligent analysis, one can say who benefited, and by how much. But does this group or this individual have a superior right to the benefits as compared with another? In the example cited above, do users of the wilderness or recreationists have a more legitimate claim to the benefits of the forest in question than the city residents whose houses might cost less if the timber were harvested? The answer to such questions obviously involves one's personal value system; not everyone will answer in the same way. What I consider as my just rights, you may consider my unwarranted privilege.

The economic welfare or equity problem is reduced, but not eliminated, if the beneficiaries pay approximately full value for the services they get. This would require that recreationists, wilderness users, wildlife enthusiasts, water users, and many other groups pay the approximate full value of the services obtained from both public and private forests. This would, of course, require major changes in relationships between forest users and forest owners. While many powerful arguments can be adduced in favor of charges on this basis, at least two objections remain: first, it will never be easy to estimate the full values of some forest uses in ways that everyone will accept; and, second, where different forest uses are incompatible, a group deprived of what it wants from the forest will generally not be fully satisfied with the fact that the other fellow is paying a full charge for what he gets. There is often a desire to obtain resources or their use which is not quieted or satisfied merely by a system of payments or charges.

## SOCIAL OR CULTURAL ACCEPTABILITY

Economic analysis of any issue of forest policy is not enough; it must be matched by a consideration of social or cultural acceptability. Men have goals, ideals, and aspirations which arise out of personal value systems, and they often choose courses of action which worsen their material situation but which produce results more nearly in accord with their value systems. So it is with forestry in the United States today. A few examples may help to make the matter clearer.

The outcry over forest aesthetics, or—more exactly—over violations of what were considered by some as forest aesthetics, is an example of a social or cultural standard. Those who are offended by large areas of clearcut timber, and/or by large volumes of low-grade or rotting logs left behind, and/or by harvested areas with rectangular boundaries which cut across natural landscape lines are not mollified by evidence that such methods of timber harvest may have been economically efficient or silviculturally desirable. They demand that timber harvest, if undertaken at all, pay more attention to the aesthetics of the situation.

Aesthetic standards vary among men. Some will be disturbed by any harvest of mature timber, rejecting arguments that the trees are likely to blow down or to succumb to insects or disease within a few years in any event. Others will be less disturbed, or not disturbed at all, by the sight of the harvested area; they may find a newly established and thriftily growing forest aesthetically more pleasing than the old one, which in their eyes had passed its prime.

Measurement of social and cultural acceptability is difficult, in part because of the variations among groups within the total society. Moreover, what is not acceptable today may become so tomorrow, and what is acceptable now may be rejected at some future date. But the forest manager who neglects social and cultural attitudes does so at his peril. Programs that are physically and biologically feasible and economically sound may founder on public attitudes.

OPERATIONAL OR ADMINISTRATIVE PRACTICALITY

A forest policy, whether implemented by public agency or by private party, must be operationally and administratively practical if it is to be successful. The test of practicality may well eliminate programs that would pass muster on other grounds.

Suppose, for instance, that it were agreed that timber cutting on private lands should be controlled by law. Suppose further that the tests of physical feasibility, economic efficiency, economic equity, and social acceptability for such a program were all passed. Would it be administratively practical to go onto every forest landowner's land, mark the trees to be cut, and enforce the harvesting limitation? What about the enormous variability among forests, to say nothing of the extraordinarily large volume of work that would be involved? In raising this "for instance," we do not, of course, mean to say that any such program would necessarily pass the tests outlined earlier in this chapter; we only say that even if it did, it might still fail operationally.

In some physical situations, carefully coordinated programs of timber harvest, timber processing, stand regeneration with improved strains, and other related programs can produce a great deal more wood from the same land area and at lower cost per unit than programs of the same kind which are undertaken more or less independently of each other. Achievement of such careful coordination among separate programs is a management task of considerable scope and complexity. Do all private firms, especially the smaller ones, have the requisite managerial skill?

For publicly owned forests, a major part of operational or administrative practicality is the appropriation process. In general, the appropriation process as it works in the federal government has been a major obstacle to the achievement of really good forestry on the national forests and other federal lands. Must this appropriation process be accepted as unchangeable, or might some modifications be made which will enable good forestry programs to be carried out better? Considerations of this kind may be fully as important as any of the earlier types of criteria for forest policy.

INTEGRATION OF VARIOUS CRITERIA

The thrust of this chapter has been the argument that *all* five criteria—physical and biological feasibility and consequences, economic efficiency, economic equity, social acceptability, and operational practicality—must be *considered* in any discussion of forest policy. The approach has intentionally been broad and eclectic, not confined to economics or any other single approach to forest policy. But how can these five kinds of considerations be integrated into a single forest policy, especially in situations when the different criteria lead to different conclusions?

First of all, it should be recognized that these five different criteria are not wholly independent of one another but are to a major degree interrelated. For instance, a program that is economically highly efficient is likely to yield large profits to someone, and this may well lead to its becoming socially acceptable when lower incomes and less profit would not have produced this result. History is full of examples of individuals or groups modifying their tastes or their standards to meet the realities of the physical or economic world. Some may deplore this, others may consider it only realism, but few can deny that it has happened. Likewise, if some policy is highly efficient economically, some means may well be found to make it operationally practical when a less efficient program might never command the managerial and organizational know-how and drive to accomplish the same operational reform. Moreover, social acceptability may depend in part upon who pays the bill: Will the advocate of forest aesthetics be as demanding if he must pay the bill as he is when the general public must pay it? Numerous other interrelationships exist among these five criteria, and those interrelationships may change over time.

The different criteria, if taken alone, may—and often will—lead to different policy recommendations. How can these five different kinds of criteria be reconciled? No means exist whereby five criteria or five relationships can each be maximized, in the mathematical sense, simultaneously. Faced with this situation, two general courses of action are possible. First, thresholds or standards for some minimum desired or demanded level of performance may be set for four of the five criteria, and then the fifth criterion can be maximized. This is essentially the process of the economist or the engineer—to the extent that either ever recognizes considerations outside his speciality. The nub of this approach is the level of the standards or thresholds for the four criteria; if very high, each may approach the level at which it would be a maximum had it been chosen as the fifth factor. By repeated recalculations, many different solutions are at least theoretically possible. This approach to forest policy formulation has its virtues, but it also has its weaknesses, not the least of which is its probable unacceptability as a process to many actors in the forest policy scene.

A different approach may be simply one of compromise; for example trading some economic efficiency for some social acceptability until some policy or package of policies is achieved which most nearly satisfies an adequate share of the concerned population. This is perhaps the politicians' approach—the search for agreement, by compromise, with explicit rejection of maximation of any single factor or criterion as an appropriate standard. But how large must the "adequate share of the population" be? And who must it be? In a great many forest policy situations, the truly general public simply does not know or care what the issues are, or what the policy alternatives may be. A selected part of the population—usually a self-selected part—tries to exert its influence and political strength, and some persons or some groups will be far more powerful than others. Is the goal a policy which most nearly satisfies the more influential group as the best attainable, or is it a policy (or policy package) which seems the least bad of the alternatives acceptable to others?

The concern of this chapter has been that all five of these criteria for forest policy be *considered* in a specific forest policy situation. After due consideration, one or more may be swept aside as relatively unimportant, or substantial agreement may be reached. The argument of this chapter rests upon two judgments of the author: that organizing policy discussion on this schema will be more efficient in resolving policy issues than will any other means of organizing such discussion, and that a policy discussion or conclusion which considers any narrower range of criteria will simply not prove viable in practice.

# 4.

## Forest Characteristics
## and Forest Uses

A great deal of variation exists among the forests of the United States. In general forests have many distinctive characteristics and are, or may be, subject to one or more different major types of use. The purpose of this chapter is to describe briefly some of the major characteristics and uses of forests, the interrelationship between characteristics and uses, and the relationships between and among the major uses.

Forests occupy a substantial proportion of the total land area of the United States—33 percent for all forests and 22 percent for the commercial forests. Forested area exceeds the area planted to cultivated farm crops, but the value of farm products as they leave the farm is roughly ten times the value of the forest products as they leave the forests. Therefore, wood production as an economic enterprise has a much lower value of output per unit of land area than farming. Wood is a heavy and bulky product; the gross weight of the timber produced is as great as that of steel, aluminum, cement, and the plastics combined, but the value is very much less. Although there is a significant foreign trade in wood products, the value of forest imports and exports is but a small fraction of the value of farm and of mine products imported and exported. Nevertheless, forestry activities are often highly important in local, rural areas; the local sawmill may be a highly important source of local employment even though the value of its output is miniscule on a national scale.

MAJOR CHARACTERISTICS OF FORESTS

Since forests are complex ecosystems, a full description of all their characteristics would be lengthy indeed. Those major characteristics of forests which affect their use for any purpose, and hence are important for forest policy, may be grouped under four headings: land, timber stand, annual growth, and annual harvest.

Land is obviously needed as a site upon which to grow trees; it is also essential for forest uses that are relatively unrelated to tree growth. In contrast to other characteristics of forests, measurement of land area presents no major problems. The multiplicity of units— acres, square miles, square kilometers, etc.—can be confusing but one kind of unit can be converted to another. Forest lands differ greatly as to soil depth and type, geological origin, fertility, slope or topography, exposure (south versus north facing slopes, in particular), climate (both macro and micro), and in other features. These land characteristics in turn affect the growth rate one may expect from various species of trees, the difficulties and costs of logging, the difficulties and rewards from uses other than timber growing, the risk of erosion, and other aspects of forest land use.

Timber stand refers to the trees now standing upon the forest land. Trees vary as to species, age, size, degree of rot or other defect, rates of growth, insect or disease infestation, and in other respects. Inventories of timber stand may take some or all of these factors into consideration. Standing timber may be classified as sawtimber or as growing stock. Sawtimbers consists of those trees in the total growing stock which are large enough in diameter, long enough to provide sawlogs within the total tree length, free enough from defect, and otherwise suitable for sawing into lumber or peeling into sheets from which plywood is manufactured. The sawlog classification is partly one of tree characteristics, partly one of technology in wood manufacture, and partly an economic one. One important consideration in management of forests is the distribution of trees in the stand by age and size. In stands where trees of all ages are intermingled on the same tract, the distribution of trees by age and size can well be measured on a particular tract. Where all trees on a tract are of the same age, distribution by age and size can be achieved only by a proper mixture of tracts of different aged trees. In either case, measurement of sawlog volume is one way—a rather crude way—of recognizing differences in age and size distribution among the trees.

In earlier decades, when an ample volume of high-grade logs existed in the woods, loggers were much more choosy about the logs they would take out than they are today, when much timber is used which once would have been left behind as waste. In the Pacific Northwest at one time, for instance, a "log" was defined as a piece of tree trunk 32 feet long, all free of serious defect, and shorter pieces were left in the woods, as unusable; today, in many areas, sound logs no longer than 8 feet are used for lumber and plywood manufacture. Some species, such as white fir and lodgepole pine, were considered unusable for lumber forty years or so ago; today they are used, though they are not considered the choicest species. At one time, sawlogs were 20, 18, 16, or some other relatively large number of inches in diameter at the small end; today, 2 x 4 studding is often manufactured out of logs no larger than 6 inches in diameter at the small end. Use of timber inventory data must, therefore, take into account the changing definitions of sawtimber.

There is one other aspect of all data relating to timber volume, whether stand, growth, or harvest, which at first glance seems a technicality that might be ignored by those interested only in the broader aspects of forestry, but which in fact is basic to all forest data and to all wood utilization data. This is whether to measure the wood volume in board feet[1] or in cubic feet (or cubic meters). To the nonforester, a further complication is the existence of several kinds of log measure—international quarter inch rule, Scribner rule, and others—but these are less important for our present concern.

A standing tree or a long cut therefrom is a cylinder, though larger at one end than at the other; boards are rectangles. The volume of the rectangles is less than the volume of the cylinder by varying amounts depending in part upon timber processing technology. Reducing the cylinder to rectangles inevitably leaves some scraps, which are increasingly being used for chips for paper and for particle board manufacture.

As long as lumber was nearly the only wood product of the forest, it was natural enough that timber stand, timber growth, and timber harvest should all be reported in board feet. When attention began to focus on wood fiber as a raw material for many uses, its total volume became the primary factor, and the form of its utilization was a secondary consideration; measures that included the whole volume of wood fiber became more relevant. Cubic feet or cubic meters is the appropriate measure for this.

An old American measure of wood volume, the "cord" of 128 cubic feet, which was originally introduced to measure fuelwood, is in modern times used to measure pulpwood. But for the old sawlog forester, the shift from board feet to cubic feet is about as traumatic as the shift from driving on the right to driving on the left would be for the average motorist. The rest of the world has been using cubic measures for a long time, but this shift has only begun in the United States; the Forest Service does not yet employ cubic feet to measure sawlogs sold from national forests.

The change in unit of measure is not merely a technical matter. It reaches to the heart of the issue: What is the wood fiber grown in

[1] A board foot was originally a piece of board 12 inches long, 12 inches wide, and an inch thick; today, in practice, those dimensions have decreased somewhat.

the forest to be used for? To the analyst, use of the cubic foot measure has the added advantage that the trees below sawlog size are included in the inventory on the same basis as the larger trees. When inventories were only in board feet, some stands of trees would appear to have an extremely rapid growth rate during a particular time period simply because a large proportion of the trees passed from just under sawlog size, where they were not counted at all, to just over that size, where they would fully enter into the inventory. If cubic foot measures also have some cutoff point, below which trees are simply not counted, the same situation may arise there. In the future, as more intensive use is made of wood grown in U.S. forests, measures of cubic volume will come increasingly to supplant measures of sawlog volume.

Annual growth of wood is a third major characteristic or attribute of the forest. It also may be measured in board feet, cubic feet, or cords; board feet measures only sawlog growth while cubic feet measures all stem growth. Some species normally grow more rapidly than do others. Growth during a year or a season may be rapid or slow, depending in part upon site qualities, weather during a particular year, and other factors. Volume of growth per tree is partly a function of the age of the tree as well as a function of site characteristics. Very young trees often grow slowly in volume though perhaps rapidly in height, younger adult trees add volume relatively rapidly, and older adult trees grow more slowly until at some age growth nearly ceases. In addition to changes in growth rate per tree, numbers of trees per acre change as the age of the stand increases; seedlings planted at 5-foot spacing would include about 1,700 seedlings per acre and a 7-foot spacing would involve 900 seedlings per acre. There is simply not enough sunlight, space for branches, soil moisture, and (perhaps) soil fertility for all of the seedlings to become large mature trees. By the time of harvest, the number of trees is sharply reduced, often to less than 100 per acre, with intervals of 20 feet or more between trees. Competition has eliminated those which could not outdistance their rivals. Under some circumstances, thinning of trees before they reach commercial size will speed up growth rates on those remaining. A later thinning of small commercial trees may yield some harvest without loss in total growth rate of the stand which remains, and such growth as does take place is concentrated on fewer and larger stems. These can more readily be harvested and would normally have a higher value than the same volume of wood in more but smaller stems. The wood gained in thinning would be lost through mortality or reduced growth anyway.

Rate of wood growth on a particular forest site is partly within man's control. Prompt regeneration of sites after harvest, fire, or blowdown will increase the average growth rate over the whole life cycle; adequate restocking to insure enough growing stems will increase the overall growth rate; planting of genetically superior strains will yield a higher growth rate than will natural reseeding of "wild" strains; in some cases, fertilization will increase the growth rate markedly; and the relationship of thinning to growth rates has already been noted. Growth rates per acre will be low when growing stands are too sparse. They will also be low when timber stands consist of large old-growth trees, with total stand volume at its maximum or nearly so, and in this case, rot, disease, death, blowdown, and other factors will remove about as much volume from the forest as is added annually by growth.

*Annual harvest* of wood is the fourth major characteristic or attribute of forests. Harvest rarely occurs equally each year on any particular site. It is more likely to be at intervals, sometimes as long as 100 or more years, sometimes as short as 5 to 10 years on a particular piece of land. Harvest is generally costly and uneconomic unless some minimum volume of wood is available for removal. An annual harvest from a forest as a whole is possible by harvesting some or all the trees on one tract this year, another next year, and so on until the harvest rotation comes back to the first site.

There are numerous and difficult technical problems in harvesting wood, especially in some areas. Roads are always needed, but their mileage and location are dependent upon the particular harvesting methods. There is danger of soil erosion and of stream pollution; the logs should be extracted with a minimum breakage and damage to the logs and to the remaining trees; and woods work has often been hazardous for the men doing it. In the long run, wood harvest cannot exceed wood growth; in the short run, harvest may exceed growth by drawing down on standing inventory. Less generally appreciated is the fact that in the long run, growth cannot exceed harvest—if we are to grow trees, we must harvest the stands making no growth so that new trees can become established and grow relatively rapidly. The vast primeval forests which covered most of the United States when white men first saw them may have been wonderful to behold, but their net growth was close to zero.

## MAJOR USES OF FORESTS

The uses of forests are numerous indeed, but I find it useful to group them into seven major categories: maintenance of an attractive forest environment, provision of opportunity for relatively intensive outdoor recreation, provision of opportunity for a wilderness experience, provision of a habitat for wildlife, watershed functions, general conservation including minimization of soil erosion, and the production of wood for various uses.[2] Each of these might be subdivided, or some might be combined, or other classifications might be employed. For each kind of use or combinations of use, there are variations in intensity of use.

Most Americans like to see, and sometimes to visit, forested areas; they like to know that forests exist. Their concern is not merely that the forests exist, but that they be attractive in appearance. This concern for an attractive forest environment ranges from casual or incidental interest by people who pay relatively little attention to forests to deep and intense concern on the part of some forest lovers. We have noted the controversies in recent years over timber harvest in general and over clearcutting in particular. Those objecting to timber harvest or its methods are concerned with maintaining an attractive forest environment. It may be, and in fact often has been, that the persons feeling strongly on the matter do not individually own the forests concerned, nor in many cases make direct personal use of them, nor directly bear any significant part of the costs of maintaining the forest in attractive appearance; yet they feel a right, as American citizens, to fight strongly for attractive forests, both publicly and privately owned ones. This "use" of the forest is in many ways illusive and difficult to measure, yet forest owners and forest managers are ill-advised to take it lightly.

Outdoor recreation is a rapidly increasing activity of most Americans. Today, the "average" American annually spends one day in a national forest, one day in a unit of the national park system, two days on a federal reservoir, more than two days in a state park, and perhaps half a dozen days in a city park, as well as additional time in other publicly or privately owned forest lands. In fact, many people do not visit these areas at all, while others go comparatively often. Total visits to public outdoor recreation areas for many years grew at about 8 to 10 percent annually. Not all of this outdoor recreation is in forested areas, but much of it is; trees add enjoyment to most outdoor recreation activities. The areas of forest used intensively for outdoor recreation are very small, but often adjacent or surrounding forested areas are used as "back country" for less intensive recreational uses, such as hunting, or provide a highly valuable total environment.

A special form of outdoor recreation—one which has aroused so

[2] Uses of forest land but not of trees are excluded; see chapter 1.

much public discussion that it seems useful to classify it separately —is the wilderness experience. Aldo Leopold, an early exponent of the wilderness classification of some national forest areas, always recognized that wilderness was both an area and a type of experience. He defined a wilderness as an area large enough to require two days by pack train to penetrate really to its core. In modern times, "wilderness" has come almost to mean any roadless area, use is often on a scale of luxury that Leopold would have found astounding and shocking, and the number of users and the scale of devotion to "wilderness" has increased by leaps and bounds. In fact, if any significant part of the original psychological experience is to be retained, wilderness use will have to be managed and curtailed in many wilderness areas, otherwise crowding will destroy the significant wilderness experience.

All forests serve as the home for wildlife. Most attention has focused upon mammals, especially the larger ones, and upon birds, but forests may be the home of various reptiles, insects, and other forms of life, and forest soils have their own microbiology, which is often important and even critical to the growth of the trees of the forest. Various forms of wildlife have different requirements for food, shelter, breeding grounds, and other aspects of the life cycle. In some forest situations, one species of bird inhabits the inner branches of the trees, near the trunk, relatively high above the ground, another species inhabits the outer edges of the higher branches, while still another lives in the tree branches nearer the ground. A mature forest may provide so little ground-level forage that deer and other grazing or browsing species find little food in it, although it may be useful for their shelter; after cutting, during the regeneration period, this same area may provide food for much larger populations of these species. It is impossible to generalize about wildlife in forests; particular species and kinds must be specified if meaningful statements are to be made about the effect of various forest practices on wildlife.

In a sense, all land is watershed, because some precipitation falls on all land (at least in the United States). Forests are important watershed areas. In general in the United States, forests grow only on areas of average to higher precipitation; the low rainfall areas of the deserts do not support forests. In interior Alaska, where evaporation and transpiration of moisture are very low, due to the short growing season and generally low temperatures, forests cover some land even where annual precipitation is less than 10 inches. Tree growth utilizes much of the precipitation which falls on forests, but runoff may be both large and important. By and large, forests are good watersheds in the sense that the forest cover keeps erosion to a minimum and sometimes helps to smooth out peaks in precipitation into more regular stream flows. Man can manipulate forest cover to favorably affect stream runoff, within some limits. By and large, reducing tree cover, either by harvest after which new tree growth occurs or by thinning out the stand, will increase runoff from forest areas. But the extent of such manipulation of forest cover to affect stream runoff is relatively modest in watersheds of any size above the smallest. More commonly, men have adversely affected watersheds by indiscriminate tree harvest and road construction, exposing large areas to accelerated runoff, clogging stream channels, and the like.

Strictly speaking, general conservation, including the minimization of soil erosion, may not be a "use" of the forest, but it is an important component of all other uses. If forested areas are to remain productive for tree growth, if they are to preserve their watershed functions unimpaired, if they are to serve as a home for a varied and numerous wildlife, if they are to be attractive areas for general viewing, intensive recreation, or for wilderness use, then it is essential that the soil and other parts of the total ecosystem be preserved from severe damage. Any use of the forest, even wilderness, constitutes some impact by man. The essential consideration is not only the severity of that impact, but the extent to which it is irreversible, or the extent to which the ecosystem can heal itself, and over what time the healing process will extend. Anyone with even the slightest acquaintance with forests realizes that most forest ecosystems have immense recuperative powers after disturbance. A wild fire, for instance, may do immense damage, yet in some years the area may be restored to a condition closely similar to that before the fire struck. For some forest types, fire at intervals is essential for forest health and reproduction. After harvest, even after one which removes all merchantable trees, plant growth of some kind quickly covers the site. The wildlife species inhabiting the forest before the harvest may have migrated elsewhere or died, but their places are likely to be taken by other species, and after some years the original wildlife composition may be closely restored. One may strive to reduce environmental impacts of man's activities on the forest and condemn actions which are needlessly destructive, and yet be fully aware of the enormous recuperative power of most forest ecosystems.

I have saved wood production for the last in my list of forest uses —not because it is least important, but because in many respects it is the most important output of the forests of the United States. Were an economic calculation made of the values of the output of all forest uses on all forests in the United States, which included generous allowances for wildlife, wilderness, recreation, watersheds, and other generally unmarketed values, I have no doubt that the value of the wood production would exceed that of all other outputs combined. This is not necessarily true for every forest. Some may have much greater value for purposes other than wood production, in part because the volume, the kind, and the quality of the wood produced annually is low and the value of other services is high; but most forests produce valuable wood and, even by the most generous calculation, relatively low values of all other forest outputs. Wood production is the purpose and objective of most forest management.

Of all the uses listed in this chapter, wood production most deserves a further categorization. Foresters recognize some 865 different species of trees native to the United States; of these, some 210 species have commercial value for their wood. In chapter 5 we recognize fourteen species or groups of species as the major forest types. These major wood sources include the southern pines, the ponderosa and sugar pines of the West, Douglas fir, and others. The wood of the various species differs in such important characteristics as specific gravity, strength of wood fibers, brittleness, ease of working, strength of boards, and others. The same species may produce rather different woods in different parts of its natural range or under different site conditions. Wood has been, and is, used for a wide variety of purposes. In the colonial and early national days, wood was almost the only basic raw material and source of fuel; later, lumber for construction was the most important wood use, and wood for ties has been a basic factor in our national railway network; still later, plywood began to be a major use of wood, especially for construction; and for the past century, wood has been the chief source from which pulp and paper were manufactured. Wood is an extremely versatile raw material, in part because there are so many kinds of wood.

In the future, wood will almost surely be increasingly viewed as a source of fiber—fiber which can be used as a base for paper, fiber which can be recombined into boardlike forms and used for construction and other purposes, and fiber which may continue to be used for plywood and lumber if these uses are more rewarding economically than use of the fiber for other purposes. In a country increasingly alert to environmental impacts and to energy supply, where real economic output continues to grow, wood is likely to assume an even larger role as a raw material than it has had in the past. The renewable character of wood, due to its growth, and the ultimate biodegradability of wood fiber combine to make it an extremely valuable and versatile raw material for the future. The production of lumber by simple sawing of logs has sometimes been attacked as a wasteful use of wood fiber, but it does have the advantage of very low energy input for manufacture. Use of wood fiber for plywood, pulp and paper, and fiberboards or particle boards requires a great deal more energy than does lumber manufacture. In addition, some of these processes now require adhesives derived from petroleum sources, although new technologies may be developed to produce the needed adhesives from wood itself.

## FOREST CHARACTERISTICS AND USE RELATIONSHIPS

The numerous and complex relationships between the forest characteristics and the forest uses are shown in table 1. Land is essential to all uses, but the requirement for land of specific types differs among the uses. For instance, wood production most needs those lands which are capable of growing wood most quickly, and this in turn has implications as to soil type, land slope, climate, and other attributes of the land. Other uses also require land but may thrive better or make better use of other land qualities.

The different uses have quite different needs for timber stand. A wilderness should ordinarily have the maximum natural stand that the site is capable of producing. The absence of man's effect upon the forest means a maximum natural stand except in those cases where the stand was temporarily destroyed or impaired by natural fires, storms, or insect or disease outbreaks, but the actual volume of this stand is unimportant—it may range from zero, for lands above timberline, to extremely high. The ordinary recreationist wants trees at the site of his active recreation, but he much prefers an open stand, with low volume per acre, to a dense one. The wood producer wants a rapidly growing stand of optimum density; this rules out both the lightly stocked stand and the mature old growth stand on which little or no new growth is occurring. The other major uses of forests have their own requirements for timber stand.

Likewise, the different uses of the forest differ greatly in their relationship to annual growth rates. Again, the wilderness use is at one extreme; if the wilderness area really has the maximum natural stand of trees, then net annual growth is zero. For all of the other major forest uses except wood production, the annual growth rate of wood is comparatively unimportant, as long as the stand is reasonably healthy. For wood production, of course, annual growth rate of wood is critical. As noted earlier, timber harvest in the long run is dependent upon timber growth—as, in the long run, timber growth is dependent upon timber harvest. If wood production is to be reasonably profitable, then wood must be grown—it is as simple as that. Production of wood from a forest has certain economic peculiarities shared by only a few other lines of economic production, such as cattle raising. The physically identical item is at the same time capital and output. The wood in the growing tree is the productive machine to which additional wood growth attaches, but the same wood is output when the tree is cut and manufactured into lumber or other wood products. A dominant fact in the profitability of wood

Table 1.   Physical Interrelations of Forest Characteristics and Forest Uses

| Forest use | Forest characteristic | | | |
| | Land area | Timber stand volume | Annual growth | Annual harvest |
|---|---|---|---|---|
| Attractive environment | Essential | Modest stand attractive; most productive stand not required | Not very important | Generally inimical, but careful planning and operation may reduce impact greatly and may enhance appearance in some instances |
| Recreation opportunity | Essential | Moderate importance; open stand often more attractive than full stand | Limited value | Possible under carefully controlled conditions and on rotation; enhances recreation opportunity in some instances |
| Wilderness | Essential | Volume at natural maximum but actual volume unimportant | Unimportant; in practice often close to zero | Unacceptable; destroys basic value of experience |
| Wildlife | Essential | Kind and numbers of wildlife responsive to stand characteristics | Limited importance | Acceptable under proper controls; desirable for some species |
| Natural watershed | Essential | Important to have good cover, but timber volume of limited importance | Relatively unimportant | Acceptable under proper controls |
| General conservation | Essential | Helpful to have good cover | Relatively unimportant | Acceptable under proper controls |
| Wood production | Essential | Thrifty growing stand essential; too small or too large volume reduces growth possibilities | Critical for long-run rate of harvest, but growth rate also dependent upon harvest | Critical both for use of wood and for its further growth |

production thus depends on the percentage rate at which new wood is added yearly; a dominant cost of further wood production is the interest on the capital that could be invested elsewhere if the merchantable tree were cut. If a stand of timber is all of merchantable size, for instance, it could all be cut, and the net income so received could be invested elsewhere; if the stand is not cut, an implicit cost for the growing of more wood in this stand is an annual interest charge on this capital. In later chapters, we shall present some data on rates of wood production in relation to wood volume in standing timber; for a large proportion of the total forested area, the rate of growth is currently very low—less than 3 percent annually. Unless growth rates, in relation to wood volume in the stand, can be increased substantially, then wood production is likely to be of dubious profitability.

One further peculiarity about this capital-output relationship should be noted: the profitability of growing does not depend as much on increases in the price of the wood harvested as one might expect. When the price of lumber or other products rises, the stumpage values of logs or trees in the woods also rise. This increases the income the wood's owner gets from sale of logs, but it also increases the value of his stand of timber, hence increases the implicit interest cost. Costs of wood growing, other than interest, may rise proportionately or not at all, hence a rise in stumpage prices is likely to leave the forest owner better off economically; but the increased profitability is vastly less than would be the case with, for instance, a wheat grower if the price of wheat rose to the same relative extent or for any other example where the same physical substance was not both output and capital.

The time frame within which forest uses are viewed is also extremely important. The interval between seeding or planting, whether by nature or by man, and later harvest of the tree for wood is long—more than a decade, usually three or four decades even for pulpwood of the faster growing species, and often a hundred years or more for some of the longer-lived species. These time dimensions of growing wood may be shortened in the future, but they will always be relatively long compared with many other economic activities. The use of the forest for purposes other than wood production also has a significant time dimension to it. A mature forest, which represents eternal majesty to someone who sees it once or once a year for a few years, may impress the forest biologist as a temporary and transitory phenomenon, for he knows that in a few decades that forest will disappear in its present form regardless of what man may do. A clearcut area may look like utter devastation to one who sees it immediately after harvest, but in a few years the site may be fully clothed with an attractive new growth.

The relatively long time span of most forestry activities requires planning and management extending over a cycle or more of change in the forest. At best, there is a considerable element of risk or of chance. The present forest may not endure forever, but just when will it change and from exactly what force or forces of change? The newly established forest may ultimately provide a timber supply, but there are many risks along the way.

The various major uses of the forest differ most of all in their relationship to timber harvest. It is critical, in the positive sense, for wood production—no harvest, no income from wood production. But it is also critical, in the negative sense, for wilderness—timber harvest, no true wilderness. For the other major forest uses, timber harvest may be favorable, or unfavorable, or endurable depending on the circumstances and on controls over methods of harvest. By and large, timber harvest of selected rather small areas favors both numbers of individuals and variety of kinds of wildlife; the openings create feed, the forest provides shelter, and the "edge effect" can be highly favorable to many species.

RELATIONSHIPS AMONG FOREST USES

Each of the various uses of the forest differs greatly in its compatibility with other uses of the forest. Wilderness use is completely incompatible with both timber harvest and intensive recreation use; or to put it the other way around, intensive recreation and timber harvest are incompatible with wilderness. Several other groupings of use exhibit differing degrees of incompatibility. Wood production, for instance, has limited compatibility with uses other than wilderness (with which it is completely incompatible), although the methods of timber harvest can often render such harvest tolerable from the viewpoint of other uses. Intensive forest recreation can also sometimes be made reasonably compatible not only with timber harvest but also with wildlife, watershed, and other uses. Compatibility of wood harvest with some other uses, such as recreation, may be achieved by staging the harvest at relatively long intervals and actually moving the other use, such as a campground, to some other site until the forest stand recovers. Likewise, intensive recreation use is likely to be compatible with other uses, including general conservation or the prevention of erosion, especially if the intensive use sites are rotated about in the whole forest. Too many human feet can in time be as destructive as a bulldozer.

Fairly high compatibility is evident between some other pairs of forest uses. Of the forty-two pairs of forest uses shown in table 2, we have classified about a fourth as "fully compatible" or "generally fully compatible," and nearly as many more as either "compatible" or "generally compatible." It should be recognized that, in some instances, the relationships will differ from those shown in the table, if a particular local situation differs from the typical situation. In some instances, different uses are not merely compatible but are also mutually reinforcing.

If wood production and harvest were subdivided according to species, size, and age of trees produced, or according to utilization of wood for lumber vs. pulpwood or other products, or perhaps in other ways, varying degrees of compatibility and incompatibility with other forest uses would be shown. These differences are often the major concern of foresters, especially industrial foresters; differences in management for wood production may make great differences in economic returns. But these are technical matters into which we do not venture in this rather general survey of forest land uses.

When two or more forest uses are fully compatible with each other, then by and large no problem of management choice between one and the other arises. It still may be that the way to maximize the output of one is not exactly the way to maximize the output of the other, but at least no outright conflict exists. When one use is completely incompatible with another, then the policy choice is at least simple: choose one, exclude the other, or perhaps divide the total forest area between the uses, but each without the other on its area. When uses are somewhat compatible, or somewhat incompatible, then choice of management techniques, including the possibility of substituting capital for labor or both for land or timber stand, assumes greater importance. In these cases of limited compatibility, the issue is not "whether," but "how much" of each and "under what conditions." While management competence and imagination are greatly needed for all forest management, they are perhaps most needed, and best rewarded, for these cases of limited compatibility. It is here that means may be found or invented to give all potential users most of what they want on economically defensible terms.

## MULTIPLE, DOMINANT, AND SINGLE USES OF FORESTS

Among a great many persons interested in forest management and use, multiple use is good (almost to the point of sanctity, for some),

Table 2. Degree of Physical Compatibility of Secondary with Primary Forest Uses

| Primary use | Secondary use | | | | | | |
|---|---|---|---|---|---|---|---|
| | Attractive environment | Recreation opportunity | Wilderness | Wildlife | Natural watershed | General conservation | Wood production and harvest |
| Maintain attractive environment | | Moderately compatible; may limit intensity of use | Not inimical to wilderness but does not insure | Compatible to most wildlife, less so to a few | Fully compatible | Fully compatible | Limited compatibility; often affects amount of harvest |
| Provide recreation opportunity | Moderately compatible unless use intensity excessive | | Incompatible; would destroy wilderness character | Incompatible for some kinds; others can tolerate | Moderately compatible; depends on intensity of recreation use | Moderately compatible; incompatible if use too heavy | Limited compatibility depends on harvest timing and intensity; roads provide access |
| Wilderness | Fully compatible | Completely incompatible, can't tolerate heavy use | | Highly compatible to much wildlife, less so to others | Fully compatible | Fully compatible | Completely incompatible, precludes all harvest |
| Wildlife | Generally compatible | Limited compatibility; use intensity must be limited | Mostly compatible though some wildlife require vegetative manipulation | | Generally fully compatible | Generally fully compatible | Generally compatible but may require limiting volume or conditions of harvest |
| Natural watershed | Fully compatible | Moderate compatibility; may require limitation on intensity | Not inimical to wilderness but does not insure | Generally compatible | | Fully compatible | Moderate compatibility; restricts harvest methods but does not prevent timber harvest |
| General Conservation | Fully compatible | Moderately compatible; if use not excessive | Not inimical to wilderness but does not insure | Generally compatible | Fully compatible | | Compatible but requires modifications in methods of timber harvest |
| Wood production and harvest | Compatible if harvest methods strictly controlled | Moderately compatible | Completely incompatible; would destroy wilderness | Compatible if harvest methods fully controlled | Compatible if harvest methods fully controlled | Compatible if harvest methods fully controlled | |

dominant use is bad, and single use is anathema. These terms have acquired great emotional overtones, but what do they actually mean?

If multiple use is interpreted to mean that every possible forest use should occur on every acre of forest land at the same time, then multiple use is impossible, has never existed in the past, does not exist today, and will never exist in the future. If multiple use means that more than one use can take place on forest land, not necessarily on every acre but perhaps on closely intermingled areas or not necessarily at the same moment in time but at various times, then multiple use is often desirable, and almost unavoidable. Land harvested for its timber is not a prime site for outdoor recreation during the harvest operations, but later it may be an excellent deer hunting site; the land reserved for wilderness use cannot also be used for timber harvest, but it may be a good watershed. Since water falls on all forested land, since all forest has some species of wildlife, and since all forest has some aesthetic qualities, then at least these functions or uses are always present, to some degree, as other uses are made of the forest.

If dominant use is interpreted to mean that some particular use of the forest completely dominates all other uses to the extent that other uses are ignored or neglected or suppressed, then most of us would reject dominant use as a forest land use principle. But if it means that one use of the forest is primary in the sense that this use provides the major purpose of the planning and management of the forest, with other uses considered and adjusted to it as far as reasonably possible, then dominant use is a sound method or objective of forest management. So defined, it approaches and grades into the second type of multiple use described above. On this basis, multiple and dominant use are not exclusive forms of forest management, but dominant use is a particular kind of multiple use.

If single use is interpreted to mean that one use, and only one use, is made of a forest to the exclusion of all other uses, then this situation is nearly always impossible. Some functions exist to some degree on all forest land, whether by neglect or in opposition to management. It would usually be impossible to eliminate all wildlife from a forest, even if it were desired to do so; likewise, all forests are watersheds in some degree; and some other uses are almost sure to be present, whether desired or not. This does not, of course, argue that such forest uses have been developed as far as reasonably possible, or that they are managed with acceptable skill and diligence.

An analysis, such as that in table 2, of the compatibilities and incompatibilities of different forest uses is far more helpful than the use of words or phrases which have come to have more than one meaning and much more helpful than a resort to slogans.

# 5.

## Variability Among Forests

Perhaps to a desk-bound, suburban living, ordinary citizen a forest is a forest is a forest, but to the forester, or indeed to any other biologist with even modest familiarity with the forests of the United States, forests differ greatly in several important characteristics. For some purposes, and in some ways, generalizations about forests, as contrasted with other major uses of land, can safely be made. But in far too many cases, someone generalizes about all forests, based upon some rather limited personal knowledge about one kind of forest. Generalizing from too narrow a base and applying to all forests conclusions which may rightfully apply to some forests, may well introduce serious error.

The forests of the United States vary in a great many different kinds of ways. We will consider only three major kinds of variability: biological, locational, and ownership variability. Complete detail about even these three kinds of variability would make this book too long. I hope that I can provide the reader with some feeling for the amounts and kinds of variation among forests and make him rather more cautious about making sweeping generalizations about all forests.

BIOLOGICAL VARIABILITY OF FORESTS

Forests differ greatly as to what they are now and as to what they can produce in the future. Ideally, our consideration of such variability should be in terms of the character or capacity of forests for each of the seven major kinds of uses of forests discussed in chapter 4. In fact, however, data for such a consideration are largely lacking. The best data—and they are far from perfect—relate to forests as producers of wood. Classifications of forests as wilderness areas, or as sites for intensive recreation, or as homes for wildlife are much less complete but some of the data collected to measure wood production characteristics are also useful for describing forests for other purposes.

First, the forester divides all forests into commercial and noncommercial categories. A full third of all forests in the United States (about 250 million acres) are classed as noncommercial. The definition of commercial forest specifies that the land must be capable of growing 20 or more cubic feet of wood per acre annually in a fully stocked natural stand. The definition gives no consideration to the value of the wood—a cubic foot of one kind of wood is as good as another for this purpose; it gives no consideration to the accessibility of the forest stand—availability of roads or cost of roads if more are needed; and it does not consider the cost of timber harvest—the distance logs would have to be hauled to market.

A great many species of trees grow to form forests in the United States. Some are the dominant species in some forests, others are one of a few major species in a forest association or complex, and others are relatively minor species in such complexes. Each species of trees has its peculiar requirement for habitat. Its ideal conditions permit its best growth, conditions somewhat less than ideal permit some growth, but in still less favorable conditions it will not grow at all. Part of each species' environment is the competition from other species for light and moisture. Presentation of data about forests is complicated by the fact that trees of some species grow in forest types dominated by other species, so that any data tabulation is somewhat a mixture of forest types and tree species. However, by far the greatest volume of the major species grow in forest types associated with the species name.

*Forest Acreages and Volumes:* Fourteen forest types, including some groupings of the less important types are considered in table 3. The two big groups are softwoods and hardwoods. Softwoods are especially useful for paper production, for lumber for construction, for plywood manufacture, and for some other special purposes. Hardwoods also have their special values, as for furniture and flooring, but are less versatile in their use possibilities than are the softwoods. The wood of each species has its own particular characteristics which greatly influence its use possibilities. Changing technologies may make some species useful for some purposes when they previously were not usable. For instance, some hardwood species are today peeled for plywood or converted into paper, which would have been impractical a decade or two ago. The acreage of hardwoods is greater than that of softwoods, but the total volume of wood and the volume per acre in the present timber stands is about twice as great for the softwoods.

Table 3. Area, Volume of Growing Stock in Stand, and Annual Growth and Removals, for Major Forest Types, 1970

| Forest type | Commercial forest area (mill. acres) | Volume of growing stock[a] | | Growing stock changes | | |
|---|---|---|---|---|---|---|
| | | Total (bill. cu. ft.) | Per acre[b] (cu. ft.) | Annual growth (bill. cu. ft.) | Annual removal (bill. cu. ft.) | Ratio of growth to removal |
| Softwoods | 207.2 | 431.9 | 2,100 | 10.7 | 9.6 | 1.1 |
| Eastern and southern: | | | | | | |
| Southern pines | 71.1 | 74.6 | 1,000 | 5.2 | 4.0 | 1.3 |
| Spruce-fir | 18.9 | 17.3 | 900 | 0.6 | 0.2 | 3.0 |
| White-red-jack pine | 12.1 | 11.0 | 900 | 0.3 | 0.2 | 1.5 |
| Other | c | 15.3[d] | c | 0.6[d] | 0.3[d] | 2.0 |
| Western: | | | | | | |
| Douglas fir | 30.8 | 105.0 | 3,400 | 1.4 | 1.9 | 0.7 |
| Ponderosa-Jeffrey pine | 28.0 | 41.0 | 1,500 | 0.6 | 0.7 | 0.9 |
| Fir-spruce | 17.8 | 58.8 | 3,300 | 0.8[e] | 0.8[e] | 1.0 |
| Hemlock-Sitka spruce | 10.8 | 60.4 | 5,600 | 0.7[e] | 1.0[e] | 0.7 |
| Lodgepole pine | 13.2 | 25.5 | 1,900 | 0.7 | 0.6 | 1.2 |
| Other | 4.3 | 23.8 | 5,500 | | | |

| Hardwoods | 266.7 | 217.0 | 800 | 7.9 | 4.4 | 1.8 |
|---|---|---|---|---|---|---|
| Eastern and southern: | | | | | | |
| Oak types[f] | 177.5 | 113.8[g] | 700 | 3.5[g] | 2.2[g] | 1.6 |
| Maple-beech-birch | 31.1 | 27.6[h] | 900 | 0.5[h] | 0.2[h] | 2.5 |
| Other | 45.2 | 56.3 | 1,200 | 2.5 | 1.3 | 1.9 |
| Western: | 12.8 | 19.3 | 1,500 | 0.5 | 0.1 | 5.0 |
| Nonstocked forest | 20.7 | | | | | |
| Total forest | 499.7[i] | 648.9 | 1,443 | 18.6 | 14.0 | 1.3 |

*Source:* U.S. Department of Agriculture, Forest Service, *The Outlook for Timber in the United States* (1973).

[a] Available data on volume of growing stock are by tree species rather than by forest type. The data here presented are our best approximation of forest type volumes. However, since some of the "types" listed contain more than one species, the figures are not always comparable and in a few cases, are omitted entirely.

[b] Rounded to the nearest hundred, because of the data limitations described in the previous footnote.

[c] Omitted because of the data limitations described in note a.

[d] Includes hemlock and cypress; these species occur intermingled in hardwood stands.

[e] Includes estimates for spruce species.

[f] Oak-hickory, oak-gum-cypress, oak-pine.

[g] Less pine volumes from oak-pine and cypress volumes for oak-gum-cypress, which are included under the other southern and eastern softwoods.

[h] Less hemlock volumes, which are included under other southern and eastern softwood.

[i] Includes 5.0 million acres in the Rocky Mountains not otherwise included due to soil, location, and other constraints.

For timber supply considerations, a more important fact than the difference in stocking rate between hardwoods and softwoods is the difference in growth rate. The average growth rate for all softwoods in 1970 was about 50 cubic feet per acre; for all hardwoods, the average rate was about 30 cubic feet per acre. Both rates reflect the history of management of these lands, and neither is nearly as high as it could be under better management and if stocking were better adjusted to wood production. All the figures in table 3 relate to actual conditions as found in 1970, including forest species and types then established on the land. In some cases, land was occupied by forest species that produce less wood per acre than other species which could be grown there. In particular, many eastern forests, both in the North and the South, had hardwood types in 1970 when pine types would produce more wood annually per acre, and, in some cases at least, the pine types were found on this land before it was cleared for farming, but it subsequently grew up to hardwood rather than to pine forest.

Among the softwoods, the southern pines—which include several different species—occupy more than a third of the total acreage but include only about a sixth of the total volume of standing softwood timber. Such pines are, in general, relatively quick-growing and trees may reach sawlog size in forty years or less, compared with 75, 100, or more years for some of the other softwood. But southern pines are relatively short-lived trees and hence do not develop large volumes of wood per acre at maturity. Southern pines have relatively high growth rates per acre on short rotations, and intensive industrial forestry has been practiced with the southern pines as much as with any species. New stands can readily be planted on abandoned cropland or on land from which trees have been harvested. Southern pines have been an especially important source of some kinds of paper but are increasingly a source of sawtimber as well as pulpwood. In 1970, more wood was being grown than was being harvested so that inventories were being built up. In any consideration of future forest production, the southern pines will surely play a major role.

Other kinds of softwood are found in the eastern half of the United States, particularly in the Northeast and in the northern parts of the Lake States. Their total acreage and their total volume of standing timber are modest, and their volume per acre was low in 1970; locally, however, they are important sources of wood.

A major species among the western softwoods is Douglas fir. Although it grows over a fairly wide area in the West, it reaches its greatest development along the Pacific Coast, especially from northern California northward. Much of the remaining mature old growth timber in the United States is Douglas fir. Average volumes of wood per acre are high—over three times the average volume in the southern pines. Well over half the total volume of sawtimber in Douglas fir in the Pacific Northwest is in trees 29 inches or more in diameter (breast high). A first-time visitor to a mature Douglas fir forest is impressed—indeed, overwhelmed—by these magnificent tall trees. Annual growth rates per acre in Douglas fir are potentially high, but now average growth is low because so many of the stands are mature and make little or no net growth. Because of the low growth rate, timber harvest substantially exceeds annual growth. However, if the comparison is limited to acreages, volumes, and growth rates on Douglas fir sites which have been harvested at some time in the past, growth rates per acre are much higher and, in total, are in excess of harvest rate on these lands.

Another major western softwood type is the ponderosa pine (together with Jeffrey, sugar, and other closely related pines). Its acreage is somewhat less than, and its total volume is not much over, a third of that of Douglas fir. Ponderosa pine forms some of the most beautiful forests in the United States—tall trees, with yellow to brown trunks, the bark typically in plates, often in somewhat open stands. It may be less impressive in size but is more beautiful than the Douglas fir or redwood. Ponderosa pine mostly grows to the east of the main Douglas fir belt, in generally somewhat drier areas. While much of this type is still in mature unharvested stands, utilization of this species has been heavy in the past. Annual harvest exceeded annual growth in 1970, in part because the growth rate was low for the mature stands. The ponderosa pine does not grow as large as the Douglas fir, yet a third of the sawtimber is in trees 29 or more inches in diameter (breast high), and almost as much more is in trees 21 to 29 inches in diameter. Thus far, ponderosa pine has not lent itself to commercial tree growing to the same degree as have the southern pines and Douglas fir, but this too is an important softwood for the future.

A western pine type deserving special mention is the lodgepole pine. It typically grows in dense stands—almost thickets—and the individual trees are often all the same age because the stand became established after a natural fire or blowdown. Individual trees generally are not large; those with diameters of 15 inches or more are relatively uncommon. For a long time its chief use (aside from its original use as lodgepoles for Indian teepees) was for railroad ties. A few decades ago it was generally not considered a sawtimber species, but it has come to be so regarded in more recent times.

Lodgepole pine is largely localized within the Rocky Mountain region. It presents special silvicultural, utilization, and management problems.

The softwoods, by and large, are in strong demand for various wood uses. For one thing, it is possible to set up a small sawmill and utilize even small local volumes of these timber types to make lumber, which will likely find a ready local market. This is not to say that every stand of softwood can be logged economically, much less to argue that all such stands should be cut. For the softwoods as a whole, growth slightly exceeds removals; for the more desirable species, log sizes, and locations, removals considerably exceed growth. This imbalance may be resolved when more old growth timber has been removed, and when vigorous new growth takes its place.

The hardwoods not only differ greatly by species, but more importantly, within most species groups there are enormous differences in tree size and quality. The Forest Service classifies somewhat more than half of the sawtimber volume of white oak and about a third that of the red oak as "select." This relatively high-grade wood is often in great demand for furniture, flooring, and cooperage, for building and industrial uses. But a substantial part of the hardwood forest acreage has relatively poor stands of trees; often they are of less desirable species, or have crooked stems, or are otherwise undesirable for wood uses, and they are generally of small sizes and small volumes per acre. For example, nearly half of the sawtimber volume in select white and red oak is in trees of less than 15 inches diameter (breast high).

The present condition of many hardwood stands is a direct consequence of their history—a history which is particularly relevant for the current discussions about clearcutting. Timber may be harvested in one of several ways: clearcut, shelterwood cut (where part of the cover is removed in one cut, the rest of the trees left to reseed the area and to shelter the young seedlings, but is later removed), selective cuts, and other methods. Each method has advantages for particular forest types and locations.

Harvest by any method may be conducted skillfully, with full consideration of the next forest to take the place of the harvested trees, or it may be conducted unskillfully, carelessly, even brutally. Much has been made—and rightly—of some of the bad examples of clearcut areas: areas left looking like battlefields with broken and scarred trunks and logs dominating the scene, perhaps with severe erosion occurring on bare soil, perhaps with delayed regeneration of a new forest. An undiscriminating and degenerating type of selective cutting is also possible, and in fact has occurred in the past on a substantial proportion of the hardwood timber stands of the South and East. A logger takes all the trees he thinks he can use with tolerable profitability, with little or no regard for what is left, and perhaps another logger, as prices have risen, repeats the process, taking still more of the growing stock. This type of "high grading" leaves undesired species, undesirable individual trees (crooked, deformed, diseased, etc.), and often damaged young trees which can never grow into desirable mature trees. This type of destructive cutting leaves standing trees on the ground, which may satisfy the undiscriminating viewer as a "forest," but it has destroyed the true forest more completely than clearcutting would have done—after the latter, an ecologically as well as an economically better forest would almost surely have grown up, than the one which occupies the land today. The present condition of a substantial part of the eastern and southern hardwoods is directly traceable to this kind of history.

The lower-grade hardwoods are not in high demand; the kind of wood found in much of the hardwood forested area of the East is not presently marketable. The large acreages, the apparent high rate of growth compared with harvest, the modestly large volume of such hardwoods are thus, to a degree, misleading. These forests are not productive of usable wood output in the same sense as are most of the softwood forests, although they may be usable forests for non-harvest purposes.

A few major forest situations in the United States emerge from the discussion to this point:

1. A large area of productive, useful, high volume softwood timber types—southern pines, Douglas fir, and ponderosa pine, especially.

2. Smaller acreages of other softwood species (lodgepole, hemlock, Sitka spruce, white, red, and jack pines, and others), some less valuable for their wood, some presenting special management problems but, in total, important for wood as for other forest uses.

3. A relatively small area of high-quality hardwoods of different species, valuable and in high demand, varying in growing conditions or in stand conditions.

4. A large area of low-quality hardwoods with stands often in poor condition and wood in low or no demand, growing much more wood than is being cut largely because lack of markets makes greater harvest uneconomic.

*Wood Producing Capacity*

Forests not only vary in their present characteristics, but also in their potential. This should also be measured separately for each of the seven major forest uses but, in practice, information is available mostly on capacity to grow wood—and even this is less detailed and perhaps less accurate than would be desirable. We have noted that foresters classify forests into noncommercial and commercial categories, the dividing line being the capacity to grow 20 or more cubic feet of wood annually. The commercial forests are further classified into five site classes on the basis of ability to grow wood in fully stocked natural stands. This classification does not measure the full potential of the forest to produce wood under improved and/or intensified forestry. Under these conditions productivity would be much greater, and it would be greater by different amounts for different types of forest.

For all commercial forests in the United States, class I sites—those capable of growing 165 or more cubic feet of wood per acre annually —include only 3 percent of the land area, but they include 7 percent of the productive capacity (table 4). Class II sites, the next most productive, include 8 percent of the area and 14 percent of the productive capacity. These two classes include the lands with deepest, most fertile soils, and with the most favorable climate. In general, prospects for continued economic wood production on these lands are good. Less productive site class III lands are far larger in area and in total productive capacity. Broadly speaking, wood growing prospects on such lands are good to fair. A still larger area with a larger total productive capacity is included in site class IV lands. These include a slightly smaller proportion of total timber productive capacity than of total forest area. In general, prospects for economic timber growing on these sites are poorer. In some cases, conversion of present hardwood stands to pine would raise the site classfication and modify these conclusions about profitability.

Of special note are the site class V forests; they include more than a fourth of all forest land but only an eighth of total productive capacity. Although these low productivity forests may have high potential for forest uses other than timber production, these lands are, by and large, marginal or submarginal for continued wood growing. Management costs of forests are often more closely related to forest area than to forest volume, and these low productive capacity forests grow slowly, often produce poorer quality trees (of each type), may regenerate slowly when cut, and otherwise simply will not repay purposeful continued forest management for wood production. I believe that the usual data on commercial forest acreages are misleading because they include so much low productivity forest.

The foregoing judgments about economic profitability of wood growing on different forest sites are based upon a site classification which employs physical rather than economic criteria. If data were

Table 4.  Area and Timber Productive Capacity, by Site Class, for Forests of Different Ownership Classes, 1970

(percent)

| Ownership class and item | Distribution by site class[a] | | | | |
|---|---|---|---|---|---|
| | I | II | III | IV | V |
| National forests: | | | | | |
| Area | 3 | 10 | 20 | 38 | 29 |
| Productive capacity[b] | 8 | 18 | 27 | 33 | 14 |
| Other public: | | | | | |
| Area | 4 | 8 | 14 | 38 | 36 |
| Productive capacity[b] | 11 | 16 | 19 | 36 | 18 |
| Forest industry: | | | | | |
| Area | 6 | 12 | 28 | 37 | 17 |
| Productive capacity[b] | 12 | 19 | 33 | 29 | 7 |
| Other private: | | | | | |
| Area | 2 | 6 | 25 | 41 | 26 |
| Productive capacity[b] | 4 | 12 | 34 | 37 | 13 |
| All ownerships: | | | | | |
| Area | 3 | 8 | 23 | 39 | 27 |
| Productive capacity[b] | 7 | 14 | 32 | 35 | 12 |

Source: President's Advisory Panel on Timber and the Environment, *Report of the President's Advisory Panel on Timber and the Environment* (1973), p. 35. Basic data from U.S. Department of Agriculture, Forest Service, "Forest Statistics for the United States, by State and Region, 1970" (1972).

[a] Site classes I to V refer, respectively to lands capable of producing growth of 165 or more, 120–165, 85–120, 50–85, and 20–50 cubic feet of timber per acre per year.

[b] Calculated by multiplying midpoint of site class interval by respective acreage.

available for an economic classification of forest sites, judgments about profitability of wood growing could be made more confidently. Differences in tree species, wood quality, location with respect to market, accessibility of a forest tract to existing roads, and other factors might modify these general conclusions when applied to specific tracts. Such modifications would raise the economic classification of some forest tracts but might well lower the classification of other tracts. The statements made here are based on the best available data and are believed to be accurate in general or in total, but they are not necessarily applicable to all forest land in each site class.

This variation in site class extends to forests in all parts of the country. Most of the site class I land is in the Pacific Northwest and California. Over 40 percent of all Douglas fir along the Pacific coast falls into site classes I and II, with only 5 percent in class V; in contrast, over half of all the lodgepole pine stands in the Rocky Mountain area falls into site class V. There is almost no site class I forest land in the North; on the contrary, by far the greater part of its forests are site classes IV and V—in today's economy, marginal or worse for continued economic wood production. But there are some good forest sites even here, so one cannot sweep away all wood production in this region as uneconomic. Their location nearer to markets for their wood gives them some advantage, and their location in a populous region gives them value for nonwood forest outputs. Many of the South's forests are classes III and IV, but there is a significant acreage of more productive forests as well as much that is poorer. The short rotations and rapid early growth of southern pines make wood growing profitable on sites of only average or slightly better productivity.

It is noteworthy that the variations in site class are fairly similar for the different major forest ownership classes. The timber industry forests have more of the better sites, while the "other private" forests have relatively less of such productive forests. There are other differences in relative amounts of each site class by ownership, but the similarities in the distribution among sites is more striking than are the differences. Each ownership group includes some highly productive land, each includes some poor forest sites. Whether one looks at tree species, forest ownership, or general region, variation in productive capacity of forests is striking, and it typically occurs within fairly short distances—soils, slopes, and other local factors are responsible.

The similarity in site distribution among different ownerships is reflected in the distribution of average productive capacity of all forests among each major forest ownership. The difference in productivity is not negligible, but it is less than is often believed to be the case (table 5). Forest industry lands have an average annual productive capacity of 12 cubic feet per acre above the average of all forests; in contrast, national forests have a productive capacity exactly equal to the average. If class V sites are omitted, the average rises for each major ownership class, by 10 to 20 cubic feet per acre, and the average differences between ownership classes shrink. Far more striking than these relatively modest differences in average productive capacity of the various forests is the very great discrepancy between productive capacity and growth actually achieved in 1970. On the average, only half of the productive capacity of fully stocked natural stands was achieved—on national forests, it was much lower. Many reasons underlie this comparatively low output. For the national forests, it is due primarily to the large acreages of mature old growth forest, on which little or no net growth is taking place; until such lands are cut, and new thriftily growing stands established, growth will remain low. In contrast, volume of growing stock on the "other private" forests has been too much depleted by past severe harvests for the forest to attain a higher present growth rate.

It would be extremely helpful if data existed on the productive capacity of forests for purposes other than wood growth—for wilderness, for recreation, for wildlife, for water yield, and for other outputs. There are some scraps of data for some areas for some of these uses—the roadless areas define the potential wilderness, water yield data per acre exist for some watersheds—but there is no comprehensive inclusive set of data for productivity of all forests, preferably by ownership classes, for each of these uses other than wood growth. One may assume, on the basis of very general knowledge, that comparable variations in productive capacity exist for these other uses, that some forests are more "productive" in some sense than are others. Equally important data would show the relationship between productivity for one use and productivity for another. In particular, to what extent may site class V lands, not well suited for wood pro-

Table 5. Productivity and Growth of Wood, by Ownership Class of Forests, 1970

| Ownership class | Estimated productive capacity[a] | | Growth achieved in 1970 on sites I–V | |
| | Land in site classes I–V | Land in site classes I–IV | Total | As percent of productive capacity of sites I–V (percent) |
| --- | --- | --- | --- | --- |
| | ( . . . . . . . . .cu. ft./acre . . . . . . . . .) | | | |
| National forests | 76 | 93 | 30 | 39 |
| Other public | 72 | 92 | 39 | 54 |
| Forest industry | 88 | 98 | 52 | 59 |
| Other private | 74 | 88 | 36 | 49 |
| All ownerships | 76 | 91 | 38 | 49 |

Source: President's Advisory Panel on Timber and the Environment, Report of the President's Advisory Panel on Timber and the Environment (1973), p. 36.

[a] Productive capacity estimated by multiplying acreage in the specified site classes (as reported in "Forest Statistics for the United States, by State and Region, 1970," Forest Service, U.S. Department of Agriculture, 1972), by the midpoint of each site class interval (taking 180 as the value for class I). Data include both hardwood and softwood forests.

duction, be productive for other purposes? To what extent can demands for wilderness be satisfied from the less (wood) productive forests rather than from class I and II sites? Much of the potential for avoiding conflict between forest uses would depend on the answer to these questions.

## LOCATIONAL VARIABILITY OF FORESTS

Neither people nor forests are distributed evenly over the surface of the United States, and the distribution of forests is considerably different from the distribution of people (table 6). On an overall average, for every citizen in our population, the forests of the nation include 2 acres of commercial forest and one acre of noncommercial forest, with growing stands of 2,000 cubic feet of softwood timber and 1,000 cubic feet of hardwood timber. But these averages are scant comfort to the person remote from a forest who seeks recreation in one, or to the poorly housed urban slum dweller who needs better housing, which, in turn, needs timber.

Commercial forest area in relation to total population is relatively high in New England, in all the southern regions, in the Pacific Northwest, and in the two Rocky Mountain regions; in all other regions, it is less than the national average. The area of noncommercial forest in relation to population is above average only in the Pacific Northwest, where the immense area of relatively unproductive interior Alaskan forests brings up the average, and in the Southwest and Rocky Mountain regions, where there are comparatively large areas of low producing forests, many of them the piñon pine–juniper types, which stretch across large areas but with scant forest cover and still lower annual growth rates.

A more than average percentage of the total land area along the Atlantic and Gulf Coasts, from Maine clear around to East Texas, and along the Pacific Coast, from Alaska through California is in forests. The Lake States, once heavily forested, now have less than an average percentage of land in forest. The great central heart of the country never was as heavily forested as the coastal regions, and more of its original forests have been cleared for farmland.

The relationship between people and timber stand volumes is different from that between people and forest area because some forests have much higher volumes per acre than do others. Only in the West—the Pacific Northwest, the Pacific Southwest, and the Rocky Mountain regions—is the volume of softwood high compared to population. This is due in part to the high volume of old-growth softwood in these regions and to the relatively small numbers of people in

Table 6. Population, Forest Area, and Timber Stand Volume, by Regions, 1970

| Region | Population (mill.) | Forest area (million acres) | | Percent of total land area in forest | Volume of growing stock[a] (bill. cu. ft.) | |
|---|---|---|---|---|---|---|
| | | Commercial | Noncommercial | | Softwoods | Hardwoods |
| New England | 12 | 32 | 1 | 83 | 20 | 15 |
| Middle Atlantic | 43 | 50 | 3 | 61 | 7 | 46 |
| Lake States | 18 | 51 | 3 | 26 | 11 | 24 |
| Central | 41 | 45 | 1 | 16 | 1 | 27 |
| South Atlantic | 12 | 48 | 1 | 65 | 19 | 28 |
| East Gulf | 11 | 41 | 2 | 60 | 19 | 12 |
| Central Gulf | 10 | 51 | * | 58 | 18 | 22 |
| West Gulf | 19 | 51 | 16 | 24 | 22 | 19 |
| Pacific Northwest | 6 | 50 | 123 | 37 | 175 | 11 |
| Pacific Southwest | 21 | 18 | 26 | 43 | 51 | 3 |
| Northern Rocky Mt. | 2 | 37 | 19 | 26 | 63 | 1 |
| Southern Rocky Mt. | 7 | 25 | 57 | 24 | 25 | 4 |
| Total | 203 | 500 | 254 | 33 | 432 | 217 |

Source: U.S. Department of Agriculture, Forest Service, The Outlook for Timber in the United States (1973), Appendix I.
Note: For the purposes of this table, the regions are defined as follows: New England—Connecticut, Maine, Massachusetts, New Hampshire, Rhode Island, Vermont; Middle Atlantic—Delaware, Maryland, New Jersey, New York, Pennsylvania, West Virginia; Lake States—Michigan, Minnesota, North Dakota, South Dakota (east), Wisconsin; Central—Illinois, Indiana, Iowa, Kansas, Kentucky, Missouri, Nebraska, Ohio; South Atlantic—North Carolina, South Carolina, Virginia; East Gulf—Florida, Georgia; Central Gulf—Alabama, Mississippi, Tennessee; West Gulf—Arkansas, Louisiana, Oklahoma, Texas; Pacific Northwest—Alaska, Oregon, Washington; Pacific Southwest—California, Hawaii; Northern Rocky Mt.—Idaho, Montana, South Dakota (west), Wyoming; Southern Rocky Mt.—Arizona, Colorado, Nevada, New Mexico, Utah.
[a] In commercial forests only.
[b] Less than one half.

much of them; but California, the most populous state in the nation now, grows a higher than average volume of softwood timber in relation to population. In contrast, the volume of hardwood in relation to population is high in nearly all the Eastern regions but very low in the West, because the West has relatively few hardwood growing areas.

All of these relationships would be different, but by varying degrees, were the definition of "commercial" forest changed to eliminate the site class V lands. A great many of the less productive forests of the Rocky Mountain regions, for instance, would be shifted from commercial to noncommercial. Relatively smaller—but still large—areas of the less productive hardwood forests throughout the East would also be shifted from commercial to noncommercial.

Within regions and states, there are strong local divergences between the location of people and the location of forests. Most people in the United States today live in cities. Although cities have trees and sometimes small forests, by and large they are not forested and cannot be, and the forests are typically some distance away. The availability of roads and of private vehicles—cars—is critical to the enjoyment of forests for outdoor recreation for most people. Location is a more important factor affecting recreation use than it is a factor affecting wood production and harvest.

DIFFERENCES IN OWNERSHIP OF FORESTS

The third major type of variability among forests concerns the ownership of forests. It is customary in the data sources to distinguish from four to six major classes of forest owners: (1) the national forests—owned by the federal government, a large and distinctive category of forest ownership; (2) other federal forests—under the management of federal agencies other than the U.S. Forest Service, each agency with its own laws and objectives, vastly smaller in total acreage than the national forests; (3) other publicly owned forests—those of states and counties for the most part, often combined with data for the federal forests other than the national forests; (4) forests owned by forest industry firms—almost always operated in conjunction with a timber processing plant of some kind; (5) forests or woods that are part of farms; and (6) other or miscellaneous private forests. Data for these latter two categories are often combined. The "other" private forests are a mixed lot, as to size of ownership unit, location, forest condition, objectives of ownership, and other characteristics; their only real distinguishing characteristic is that they do not belong in any other ownership group.

Some aspects of these ownership classes are readily observable and measurable and are considered in this section. The most important differences are in the objectives and purposes of ownership, and these are harder to describe accurately and to measure quantitatively. The national forests were established and have been continued out of a concern for future timber supply and for watershed protection. Conservation of the forest resources, sustained yield forestry, and multiple use management are deeply ingrained in Forest Service policy (or ideology) and were given legislative expression in the Multiple-Use Sustained Yield Act of 1960. Silvicultural considerations have loomed large in national forest administration. In recent years, more concern has been given to broad ecological relationships than formerly was the case, but national forest administration has never given more than limited attention to economics —the national forests were not established to earn a profit. The other publicly owned forests, some federal and others state or local, have somewhat the same objectives as the national forests, but more attention has been given in some, especially in state forests, to current earnings from forest management.

Forest industry forests are owned in the expectation of making a profit from wood growing and wood processing. The total operations of such firms are very much subject to the tests of economic efficiency and business profitability. Woods operations are expected to be profitable, either when considered separately or as a source of supply for the processing establishment. As noted earlier, forest industry forests on the whole tend to be on somewhat more productive sites than other forests; but, as also noted earlier, great variations in productivity occur among other forests. Some critics of forest industry forest management would argue that the industries have had too short a time horizon, have given inadequate thought and consideration to their future supply of wood, and have given inadequate attention to the values of the forest other than wood production. Forest industry firms, on the average, practice more intensive forestry for wood production than do other owners, and as a result grow more timber per acre annually and grow more timber in relation to productive capacity.

The farm woods or forests are nearly all incidental to the production of cultivated crops and of domestic livestock. In many parts of the United States, cropland and land suitable for forests but not for cultivated crops are closely intermingled. When he acquires enough cropland for efficient farming, the farmer may also acquire a good bit of wooded area. By and large, the management of these farm woodlots has not been intensive or even deliberate. In many cases, the woods are cut when the farmer needs money and an opportunity presents itself to sell timber; otherwise they are largely neglected. The "other private" owners are a highly varied lot, as noted. Some own forest land as a place for personal recreation; others because they like to manage a small forest and work in it themselves as a hobby; still others acquire land as a speculative investment; some inherit forested land and postpone selling for sentimental reasons. Some businesses own forest land as an incident to their main activity; for instance, several electric utilities and some railroads own some forest because the land is watershed or for some other reason is associated with their main activity. Various studies seem to indicate that many small private forest owners are not much concerned about immediate income from their properties, and their objectives are something other than income maximization from the forest.

Of the total commercial forest area in the United States, nearly 60 percent is farm and "other" (table 7); the next largest ownership class is the national forests, followed by the forest industry forests. If one considers only those commercial forests which have harvestable sawtimber on them (excluding commercial forests with timber of smaller sizes), the distribution is somewhat different. For all forests, 43 percent of the commercial acreage contains sawtimber stands; for national forests, the proportion is well over half; for the forest industry forests, about half; and for the "other" category, well below average. Still another measure is the area of commercial forests with more than 5,000 board feet of standing sawtimber per acre. These relatively heavily stocked stands are somewhat more than half of all sawtimber stands and somewhat more than a fifth of all commercial forests. The proportion of acreage in this category is very much above average for the national forests, somewhat above average for the forest industry forests, and very much below average for the "other" forests. In part, this reflects forest type, since some types normally have higher volumes than others, but mostly it reflects the relative amounts of mature old growth timber in each ownership category.

The volumes of growing stock and of sawtimber for the various ownership groups tell a still different story. For the softwoods, the national forests are dominant—slightly more than half of the total volume of all softwood sawtimber is found on the national forests, even though they are only 18 percent of all commercial forest land in the country. For hardwoods, the "other owners" are dominant. A great deal of the hardwood on these "other" ownerships is in small trees, often of poor varieties, often of poor quality; and though they contain a considerable volume of wood in the physical sense, its economic value is very low.

Table 7. Area of Commercial Forest, Volume of Growing Stock, and Volume of Sawtimber, by Major Ownership Groups, 1970

| Ownership class | Area of commercial forest | | | Total volume of growing stock (...bill. cu. ft....) | | Total volume of sawtimber (...bill. bd. ft....) | |
|---|---|---|---|---|---|---|---|
| | Total (......million acres.........) | Sawtimber stands | Stands with more than 5,000 bd.ft. per acre | Soft-wood | Hard-wood | Soft-wood | Hard-wood |
| Federal: | | | | | | | |
| National forests | 92 | 54 | 45 | 200 | 18 | 982 | 42 |
| Other | 15 ⎱ | 18 | 12 | 48 | 20 | 223 | 42 |
| Other public (state, local) | 29 ⎰ | | | | | | |
| Forest industry | 67 | 32 | 18 | 73 | 27 | 318 | 68 |
| Farm | 131 ⎱ | 111 | 38 | 110 | 153 | 382 | 366 |
| Other private | 165 ⎰ | | | | | | |
| Total | 500 | 215 | 113 | 432 | 217 | 1,905 | 515 |

Source: U.S. Department of Agriculture, Forest Service, *The Outlook for Timber in the United States* (1973), pp. 231–47.

All of the foregoing discussion is in terms of the current definition of "commercial" forest. If the site class V forests were no longer considered commercial, as I have suggested, the picture would change somewhat.

The acreage in farm forests declined about 40 million acres from 1952 to 1970, while the acreage in "other" ownerships increased nearly as much. This largely reflects farm consolidation, farm abandonment, and land purchase by nonfarmers in various parts of the country where small farm forests were most common. In 1952 there were reported 3.4 million farm forest owners; today, the figure cannot be over 1½ million—perhaps no more than 1 million—because of extensive farm consolidation and abandonment. Even at the smaller figure, the average farm woodlot or forest has only 131 acres —an area far too small for much efficient forest operation. Judging by the Census of Agriculture, less than half—perhaps less than a fourth—of these farm owners sell any forest products from their land in any particular year, although over a period of years perhaps all of them make some sales. In 1952, there were 1.1 million "other" owners; this number has probably been increasing, as larger and larger numbers of city people have bought rural, forested land for recreation or other purposes. The average size of these forest ownerships is probably not much different than that of the average farm woodlot.

Most farmers find that the best use of their available time and managerial capacity is in activities other than woodlot management, and the latter gets only sporadic and incidental attention in many cases. For all "other" ownerships, sales of timber products are likely to occur only at intervals. In any one year, many owners will seem indifferent to cash income from timber sales, but over a long period of years or their whole lifetime, sales may average out at a modestly high level per acre.

These data on total acreages and total volumes are more readily understandable if put in terms of ratios; this has been done for softwoods in table 8. The per acre volume of standing timber, whether all growing stock or sawtimber, is very high on national forests, reflecting primarily the large acreages of mature old growth timber on the national forests. The per acre volumes are not far from average for the other public forests and for the forest industry forests; they are far below average on the "other" private forests, reflecting their current low stocking, which in turn reflects their past heavy harvesting.

The data presented in this chapter make clear the great importance of the national forests in the total U.S. forest situation: they include a large area of forest land, half the total sawtimber volume, and a

Table 8.  Volume, Growth, and Harvest Relationships for Softwood Timber, 1970

| | National forests | Other public forests | Forest industry forests | Other private forests | All forests |
|---|---|---|---|---|---|
| Volume of growing stock per acre, cu. ft. | 2,990 | 2,230 | 2,010 | 1,340 | 2,080 |
| Volume of sawtimber per acre, bd. ft. | 14,700 | 10,280 | 8,740 | 4,650 | 9,180 |
| Annual growth: | | | | | |
| Growing stock per acre, cu. ft. | 31 | 45 | 70 | 62 | 52 |
| Growing stock, as percent of standing volume | 1.0 | 2.0 | 3.5 | 4.6 | 2.5 |
| Sawtimber per acre, bd. ft. | 129 | 183 | 273 | 216 | 195 |
| Sawtimber, as percent of standing sawtimber volume | 0.88 | 1.78 | 3.13 | 4.63 | 2.11 |
| Annual harvest: | | | | | |
| Growing stock per acre, cu. ft. | 31 | 34 | 85 | 45 | 46 |
| Growing stock as percent of standing volume | 1.0 | 1.5 | 5.2 | 3.4 | 2.2 |
| Growing stock as percent of growth | 101 | 76 | 121 | 73 | 90 |
| Sawtimber per acre, bd. ft. | 191 | 196 | 448 | 176 | 230 |
| Sawtimber as percent of standing volume of sawtimber | 1.3 | 1.9 | 5.1 | 3.8 | 2.5 |
| Sawtimber as percent of growth of sawtimber | 148 | 107 | 164 | 81 | 119 |

Source: U.S. Department of Agriculture, Forest Service, The Outlook for Timber in the United States (1973), pp. 231–33, 240–47, 273–81.

61

large productive capacity. Their multiple use management gives major attention to forest outputs other than timber. Moreover, as publicly owned property, their management is necessarily public business, in which all citizens can reasonably have an interest and an input. Because of their large volume of standing sawtimber, the national forests can be an unusually important source of lumber and other products in the next several years. For all of these reasons, special attention in this book is directed toward the national forests.

There is a substantial correlation between region and ownership which affects public policy on forest issues. The national forests, especially those with large timber volumes, are in the West, and are a matter of particular concern for western people and their elected representatives. The small private forests are dominantly in the East, both northern and southern sections, and are of particular concern to people in these regions and to their elected representatives. For instance, measures to provide federal aid to small private owners will command special attention from southern Congressmen and Senators. Forestry programs have a better chance of enlisting support from several regions if they include something for each type of ownership.

This chapter may well end where it began: for some purposes it is legitimate to refer to "forests" in the same sense that it is legitimate to refer to "schools" or to "industry" or to "automobiles," but for many purposes it is necessary to be more specific. Considering forest types, regions, forest ownerships, site productivity classification, and differences in timber stand type and volume, there are probably 4,000 significantly different forest situations in the United States—significantly different for economic analysis, silvicultural practice, social objective, or other reasons. An overmature lodgepole pine forest heavily infested with dwarf mistletoe is as different from a thrifty young artificially planted southern pine forest as a piece for the carburetor of a 1960 Ford is from a piece for the transmission of a 1973 Chevrolet—each forest is a pine forest, as in the other case each part belongs to an automobile, but in neither case is one interchangeable for the other. If there is to be sensible debate on forest policy, then we must distinguish and specify which type of forest we are talking about.

# 6.

## Physical and
## Biological Feasibility
## and Consequences

It is physically and biologically possible to do a great many things
in and with the forests of the United States, if one does not count
the costs or consider the impacts of some particular line of action on
other outputs and uses of the forest. We really do not know the limits
of what is physically and biologically possible with our forests because we have never expended much effort in trying to measure or
estimate such potentiality. Particular management actions have
physical and biological consequences in terms of later timber stand
and later forest use that are not always well understood in advance.
In this chapter, as in most others, the discussion should consider
separately each of the forest uses, but—as elsewhere—the best information (though imperfect) is for wood production.[1]

WILDERNESS USE OF FORESTS

The area and amount of wilderness use of which American forests
are physically and biologically capable depends upon how fussy one
is in defining both the wilderness experience and the wilderness
area.

The type of wilderness as found in North America by the invaders
from Asia 13 to 20 thousand years ago, or by the European explorers
300 to 500 years ago, or by Lewis and Clark in their explorations
about 170 years ago, or by John Wesley Powell along the Colorado
River 100 years ago, is no longer found in the United States today.
All areas of the United States have been explored, all have been
mapped in some degree, nearly all have trails (or portages) which
cross them. Wilderness travel along these trails today is very much a
powder puff operation by explorer standards. To no small degree,

---

[1] For reasons outlined in chapter 1, we do not consider in this chapter grazing of
domestic livestock, mineral extraction, transportation, and residential uses of forest
land.

travellers in the "wilderness" today play-act, by climbing mountains, or running rapids in canoes, or exploring caves, or undertak-
ing some other activity not really necessary to their travel through
the wilderness, but which helps them to imagine they are indeed in
an unexplored wilderness. Much recreation, even such sedentary
forms as watching TV or reading mystery stories, is also play-acting;
imagination may lift one from the tensions and cares of ordinary life
and hence be highly advantageous to emotional health.

In the United States today, there is much glorification of the
"wilderness," but it is a wilderness which is fast changing. Its very
popularity and the resulting volume of visits are destroying much of
the character of the wilderness as it existed no more than a decade
ago. Too much use by too many people is a greater threat to most
wilderness areas today than is the chainsaw. More of the wilderness
experience can be preserved by more and better management of such
areas than by letting their use increase without control. In some
wilderness areas, it would be possible to open up new routes for
travel, thus diluting some of the present concentration of use and
separating users by some distance. Careful scheduling of parties
would reduce encounters with other people along the trail, thus
preserving the illusion and perhaps the fact of solitude for those
travelling the trails. It would be possible to reduce or at least not to
allow increases in the "catered wilderness" travel, in which large
parties travel in relative luxury through wilderness areas. In the end,
some control over numbers of wilderness users will be necessary.
Unless some or all of these measures are adopted, and rather soon,
the wilderness areas of the past and even those of the present will
disappear—"loved to death" by their avowed friends.

Various estimates have been made of the potential wilderness area
of the United States, but most such estimates do not separate forested
from nonforested areas. In 1972 the Wilderness Society suggested
there were 269 potential wilderness areas (table 9). In 1972 the
Forest Service identified and had under study some 1,442 areas
within the national forests; each of these areas had 5,000 or more
acres of roadless land (table 10). It is notable that, of the 55 million
acres within such areas, only 18 million acres are considered commercial forest; this is about 20 percent of the total commercial forest
area of the national forests. Although information is not available, it
is probable that much of this is site class V forest; if it consisted of
only site class V land, it would be nearly three fourths of the total
class V land in national forests. The annual allowable harvest from
these lands has been estimated at 2.2 billion board feet annually, or
about 15 percent of the presently estimated sustained yield cut of the
national forest system. In thus identifying these areas for initial

Table 9. Present and Potential Units of the National Wilderness
Preservation System

| Status and administering agency | Number of areas | Gross acreages |
|---|---|---|
| 1. Present units in National Wilderness Preservation System: | 85 | 10,445,148 |
| Forest Service | 62 | 10,258,036 |
| National Park Service | 2 | 93,503 |
| Bureau of Sport Fisheries and Wildlife | 21 | 93,609 |
| 2. Potential units proposed for National Wilderness Preservation System: | 184 | 58,673,457 |
| Under review by agency or Congress | 157 | 56,783,447 |
| Forest Service | 27 | 4,331,156 |
| National Park Service | 59 | 27,219,288 |
| Bureau of Sport Fisheries and Wildlife | 71 | 25,233,003 |
| Subjects of proposed legislation but not recommended by an agency or the President | 27 | 1,890,010 |
| Forest Service | 27 | 1,890,010 |
| Total present and potential units: | 269 | 69,118,605 |
| 3. Roadless area review of Forest Service | 1,442 | 55,292,631 |
| (Commercial forest acreage) | | 18,292,631 |

Source: President's Advisory Panel on Timber and the Environment, Report of the President's Advisory Panel on Timber and the Environment (1973), p. 521. Basic data (items 1 and 2): from The Wilderness Society, 1972, as of Aug. 30, 1972; (item 3): from U.S. Forest Service, special communication to the President's Advisory Panel, Oct. 13, 1972 (preliminary data).

study, the Forest Service made no commitment that all were suitable for wilderness designation or for detailed study. In October 1973, the Forest Service announced that 274 of these areas (12 million acres) would be intensively studied for possible inclusion in the wilderness system. The agency's action almost surely does not settle finally all controversy over national forest wilderness areas.

A still different approach yielded an estimate of slightly more than 70 billion acres as the potential dimension of the wilderness system in the United States on all federal lands; only 21 million acres of this were in national forests (table 11). Some of this area might, upon critical examination, be excluded as not suitable for wilderness designation, and much of the area in this latter estimate is not forested.

These various sources of data apply to areas recognized as still wilderness, in some sense. They lack roads, have not been logged, and have virtually no permanent residents today, although most have been and are today in some cases open to mineral exploration and grazing by domestic livestock. Of more questionable character

Table 10.  All Roadless Areas on National Forests

| Region[a] | Number of areas | Total land (.......acres.......) | Commercial forest land | Potential yield (....thous. bd. ft.....) | Annual allowable harvest |
|---|---|---|---|---|---|
| 1 | 273 | 7,865,738 | 4,710,745 | 1,899,429 | 463,760 |
| 2 | 250 | 5,517,615 | 2,240,256 | 531,607 | 118,654 |
| 3 | 88 | 1,188,426 | 160,314 | 53,776 | 47,246 |
| 4 | 437 | 11,465,283 | 3,641,821 | 497,147 | 174,892 |
| 5 | 128 | 3,070,460 | 717,849 | 209,110 | 209,110 |
| 6 | 256 | 5,585,776 | 3,150,265 | 763,730 | 696,330 |
| 8 | 2 | 36,935 | 23,321 | 1,858 | 360 |
| 9 | 0 | 0 | 0 | 0 | 0 |
| 10 | 7 | 20,553,910 | 3,647,700 | 1,169,030 | 579,589 |
| ITF | 1 | 8,488 | 422 | 359 | 0 |
| Total | 1,442 | 55,292,631 | 18,292,693 | 5,126,046 | 2,289,941 |

Source: From U.S. Forest Service, special communication to the President's Advisory Panel on Timber and the Environment, Oct. 13, 1972 (preliminary data).

[a] Region 1 is the Northern Region; 2, the Rocky Mountain; 3, the Southwestern; 4, the Intermountain; 5, California; 6, the Pacific Northwest; 8, the Southern; 9, the Eastern; 10, Alaska; and ITF, the Institute of Tropical Forestry in Puerto Rico.

in the minds of many people are areas in the eastern United States from which the original forest has been cut, perhaps some of the land cleared, where roads have existed or exist today, where perhaps a few persons still live. These areas have now grown up once again to forest and are, or could be in a relatively few years, a reasonable facsimile of a wilderness—or of a modified wilderness, or of a quasi-wilderness, or a restored wilderness, whatever term one prefers. To the purist or according to the Wilderness Act of 1960, which defines wilderness as "an area where the earth and its community of life are untrammeled by man, where man himself is a visitor who does not remain—without permanent improvements or human habitation—imprint of man's work substantially unnoticeable . . . ," such areas are not wilderness and never can be—their virginity has been lost forever. Others, including many persons properly identified as wilderness advocates, are little concerned with the history of an area but focus on its present condition or even upon the condition to which it could be restored. To the average user, many eastern areas could be brought to resemble a wilderness; at the least, they could be preserved as relatively unmodified forest areas, available for a certain type of outdoor recreation. The present lack of such areas in the East and South would make all future areas of this type particularly valuable.

How far will present standards of wilderness endure, and how far will they be modified? In particular, will the supporters of wilderness at some future date modify their standards downward and seek

Table 11. Potential Dimensions of the National Wilderness Preservation System

| Agency | Acreage under study as wilderness (mill.) | Assumptions regarding eventual wilderness classification (percent) | Acreage assumed to be classified as wilderness (mill.) |
|---|---|---|---|
| Forest Service, total[a] | 23.8 | | 20.9 |
| Wilderness (currently in National Wilderness Preservation System) | 9.9 | 100 | 9.9 |
| Primitive (awaiting review)[b] | 4.4 | 100 | 4.4 |
| De facto (48 States) | 7.0 | 67 | 4.7 |
| De facto (Alaska) | 2.5 | 75 | 1.9 |
| National Park Service, total[c] | 27.3 | | 20.1 |
| 54 units in 48 States and Hawaii | 19.8 | 67 | 13.3 |
| 3 units in Alaska | 7.5 | 90 | 6.8 |
| Bureau of Sport Fisheries and Wildlife, total[d] | 26.9 | | 22.5 |
| Acreage to be reviewed, exclusive of Alaska | 3.1 | 50 | 1.6 |
| Acreage to be reviewed in Alaska | 22.6 | 90 | 20.3 |
| Acreage already reviewed, exclusive of Alaska | 1.1 | 50 | 0.5 |
| Acreage already reviewed in Alaska | 0.1 | 100 | 0.1 |
| Bureau of Land Management, total[e] | 11.0 | | 8.0 |
| Study areas in 48 States | 2.2 | 67 | 1.4 |
| Study areas in Alaska | 8.8 | 75 | 6.6 |
| Total, all agencies | 88.5 | | 71.5 |

Source: G. H. Stankey, "Myths in Wilderness Decision Making," *Journal of Soil and Water Conservation*, 26(5), pages 184–188, as reproduced in President's Advisory Panel on Timber and the Environment, *Report of the President's Advisory Panel on Timber and the Environment* (1973), p. 523.

[a] Assumptions regarding the percentage of Forest Service "de facto" acreage to be classified as wilderness are arbitrary ones that attempt to take into account the demands for a growing wilderness-user population, other resource demands, and the availability of lands to meet this demand.

[b] Additions to primitive areas in the reclassification process have averaged about 25 percent. However, these additions are taken from land classed above as "de facto" wilderness.

[c] The two-thirds assumption for national park units outside Alaska is probably an overestimate. Of the 17 units studied to date, preliminary wilderness proposals have averaged 54 percent. The 90-percent assumption for Alaska was made in light of the low level of development and light use pressures.

[d] The Bureau of Sport Fisheries and Wildlife has reviewed 30 areas in the United States, exclusive of Alaska. At present, wilderness recommendations average 45 percent of gross acreage. In Alaska 76,000 acres have been reviewed; virtually all (99.9 percent) have been recommended for wilderness. It has been assumed that prior developments and wildlife management needs would allow for a 90-percent withdrawal of the remaining acreages.

[e] There is virtually nothing available from which assumptions regarding Bureau of Land Management withdrawals for wilderness proposals could be made. The two-thirds figure for the forty-eight states and 75 percent for Alaska attempt to recognize, as do the assumptions on "de facto" Forest Service acreage, the competing resource demands and the alternative sources of supply for these sources.

to have additional areas, other than those included in any of the sources used in this section, also reserved as wilderness? One simply cannot know. Experience with the Wilderness Act of 1964 may or may not be illuminating. When that Act was under consideration by the Congress, its supporters in Congress and outside made much of the fact that they were not asking for any new wilderness areas—they wanted only legislative protection for areas then designated as wilderness by Executive action. Within much less than a decade, this position was modified, with the result that some hundreds of areas are now urged for wilderness designation. This is partly a shift in political position but also partly a redefinition of wilderness. May we some day see another major attempt to greatly broaden the definition of wilderness?

RECREATION

The physical possibilities for outdoor recreation in the forests of the United States depend upon (1) how far people are willing to travel for such recreation, (2) what kinds of activities they prefer or demand, (3) what kinds of equipment they wish to use, (4) what seasonal use patterns they will insist upon, and (5) how much crowding they are willing to tolerate at the recreation site and on the road to and from. If one takes a relaxed or generous definition or attitude toward each of these constraints, then the *physical* possibilities for outdoor recreation in a forest setting are very great indeed.

In 1965 The Bureau of Outdoor Recreation estimated that over 520 million acres (all physical types of land, all ownerships) were "recreation lands." These data have severe limitations for our purpose: the definition included the entire area of the national forests, much of the land administered by the U.S. Bureau of Land Management (BLM), the national park system, the state parks, some other public areas, and about 30 million acres of private land. Aside from the fact that a large proportion of this land is not commercial forest, the extent of the recreation "use" is very limited on much of it. Nearly all national forest and much privately owned forest are open to recreation in the sense that people may hunt over the land or hike through it, but in many instances they would have to force their way through dense forests or underbrush, and only a few hardy individuals would do that. In fact, by far the greater part of the total recreation visits to forests of any ownership class takes place along roads and trails, along streams and around lakes, or within relatively short distances of these; relatively few of the total number of visitors are willing to walk very far from their car. We know that the total number of recreation visits to all state parks equals or exceeds the number of recreation visits to all kinds of federal land, and the state parks in 1970 included only about 7½ million acres of land.

The physical possibilities of developing campgrounds, picnic areas, and other intensive recreation use sites (including playgrounds, golf courses, swimming pools, and other intensive "urban" type areas) on forest lands of the United States are very great indeed —if one ignores cost, alternative uses, locational, and other restraints. Vast acreages of forest now in private ownership, including much of that in "other" ownership, could be subdivided into 10, 5, or even 1 acre parcels for ownership and use by private parties for recreation, and the area could still be "forest" in a sense.

If one has little or no concern for the quality or character of the recreation area, if people would be willing to use some forested areas during a longer season, and if more people would travel farther from their homes to a forest recreation area, then the number of visitor days in outdoor recreation that could be accommodated in all forest settings in the United States would be so large as to be meaningless. The constraints on outdoor recreation use of forests are more than physical capacity; they must also include the impact of recreation upon other uses of the forest, and the impact of increasing numbers of people upon the quality of the recreation experience.

WILDLIFE

We have previously pointed out that it is unsafe to generalize about wildlife, since environmental conditions favorable to one species may be highly unfavorable to another, and this stricture is appropriate here. The physical and biological possibilities for increasing the numbers of some wildlife species in a forest setting are generally very great if cost is no object, and if impacts on other forest uses are disregarded. But for some other species, it would be difficult to increase numbers very much no matter what one was willing to do. The ivory-billed woodpecker lived (or lives, if it still exists) in undisturbed virgin forest, or a reasonable facsimile thereof, and such a forest cannot be created overnight—if at all—regardless of willingness to spend money.

When one considers the physical and biological potentiality of wildlife in forested areas, or indeed in any areas, several questions arise. How far should the wildlife live in wholly natural conditions, and how far should they be assisted by man? More specifically, do we feed game animals, such as elk, in the winter, or do we let some of them starve? Do we hunt animals, killing some, or do we let them reproduce beyond their feed supply, letting some starve, and in the process destroy some of the productive capacity of the forest to support that species? Do we protect only the "nice" wild animals, or do we protect the predators too? Protect only the deer and the antelope, or the coyote and the grizzly bear too? While there are technical considerations involved in answering each of these questions, the basic consideration is man's social or cultural environment. What do we want, and how much do we want it? The answer involves economic and social considerations, which are discussed in later chapters.

A specialized segment of the foregoing is the question of what to do about endangered species, and how great an effort to make in their preservation. Is it a reasonable goal to seek to preserve every species of wildlife that now exists in the forest? Less than 10 percent, perhaps no more than 1 percent, of all species of living things which have existed since life first began still remain on earth; the others have become extinct, often with little or no interference by man. When most people talk about endangered species, they have in mind mammals and birds and often only the larger species of each; fish and reptiles are mentioned only infrequently, and insects and microbiologic organisms will rarely be considered, even though the health of the forest may depend very much upon their contribution to its soil microbiology. What is it worth to the nation to preserve the whooping crane (not a forest species) or the ivory-billed woodpecker (if indeed it still exists)? Is money, manpower, and managerial competence better spent here than in some other aspect of natural resource management?

The number and variety of wildlife species and the numbers of individuals in each species in any generally forested setting are very much under the control of man in the United States today. Substantial proportions of all forest wildlife are "edge" dwellers, who benefit from the existence of an edge between forest and nonforest; the latter areas often provide the feed, with the forest providing the shelter. This is especially true for all animals which graze grass or similar feed or which browse upon shrubs—deer, particularly, but many others, including rabbits and other small animals; where these animals are found, their predators will also be found, unless man interferes too much. Likewise, many kinds of birds thrive along forest edges, living partly in the forest, partly in the clearing, or in both. Because of this edge effect, timber harvest may be beneficial to the variety and numbers of wildlife. This depends in part upon keeping the individual areas of timber harvest relatively small (50 acres or less) and also, at least in some cases, upon conscious steps to increase wildlife food species in the clearings. Harvest of old growth timber will increase the numbers of many kinds of wildlife.

There are other wildlife species which dwell in the deeper forests or which require the maintenance of certain types of trees as sources of food and as places for their homes. Squirrels, for instance, may live on oaks and other tree species which produce food for them; they and other wildlife species may live in cavities in the trunks of some kinds of trees. In some hardwood stands, dead trees can be preserved or trees not suitable for timber harvest can be girdled to produce dead trees, in which many kinds of wildlife can find homes. Wildlife species vary greatly in their ability to migrate quickly; if their forest home is cut in a timber harvest, some species can move quickly to other sites, while other species move less easily and the impact of the timber harvest is greater. In areas where timber is normally harvested by clearcutting in patches, deer and other species rather quickly move to recently harvested areas where the food supply is greatest, and hunters find such areas their best hunting grounds.

The physical and biological possibilities of managing forests to preserve or increase either the variety or numbers of wildlife are very great, and they vary from one forest situation to another. A major difficulty is that the private forest owner has no economic incentive to provide for wildlife, since any value he creates is captured by others. Even on publicly owned forests, wildlife makes no monetary return to forest management, but wildlife management involves costs. A forest policy issue, therefore, is how to get consideration for wildlife more deeply ingrained into the planning and the management of the forest, especially the planning and management of timber growing and harvest.

WATER

Water flows naturally from almost all forests where man's influence is negligible. How far are these natural flows the standard for quantity, seasonality of flow, water quality, water temperature, and other aspects of stream flow which should be applied to managed forest areas? If this natural flow is accepted as the standard or desideratum to be sought, then the physical possibilities of forests as watersheds are limited to achieving or approaching this standard. In particular, forest use must be managed to reduce its impact upon stream flow. For wood harvest, this means careful control over methods of logging; for all uses, it means careful control over mileage, grade, cut and fill, and other aspects of roads; for recreation, it means limiting the intensity of use to what the soil and the vegetation can stand; and so on. It may be impossible—even with the greatest care and with unlimited expenditures of time, effort, and money —to avoid *any* impact upon stream flow if man invades a forested area in any significant way. By careful management, impacts may be kept very low, probably tolerable for most stream uses including fish reproduction.

If one does not accept the natural stream flow as the objective of forest watershed management, but seeks more water or a different seasonal distribution of flow, then some modest physical possibilities exist. In some situations, cloud seeding may increase rainfall or snowfall, and the watershed may require management to accommodate the large runoff without damage. By reducing the amount of deep-rooted vegetation, such as trees, and substituting shallower-rooted vegetation such as some shrubs and grasses, the transpiration from the area may be reduced and the stream flow increased without causing increased soil erosion. By cutting trees in strips or patterns, it may be possible to influence snow accumulation on some watersheds and thus affect the timing of snow melt and the timing of stream runoff. By modest physical structures, such as terraces where topography and soil permit or low checks in the stream channel itself, the amount and timing of the runoff can be modified. The total effect of such watershed measures is often modest. Cutting trees in a clearcut or other method of harvest often increases water yield considerably for a few years, but an increase of as much as 20 percent in the total stream runoff on a continuing basis is as much as can be expected in most cases, and sometimes the effect will be distinctly less. Such added flows of water will often be costly, both in terms of direct expenditures of manpower and money and in terms of income foregone from wood production. Under existing water law in most states, the landowner, whether federal government or private firm, would have great difficulty in capturing the value of the added water production.

Wood production, which is careless of the effect on watershed, may modify the natural stream flow of the undisturbed forest considerably and in a way that most people would consider undesirable. Harvesting of large areas of forest in a single watershed, by almost any means of harvest, is likely to increase stream flow, sharpen the seasonal peak of flow, result in warmer water, increase the sediment and chemical content of the water, and perhaps have other effects as well. Logging which involves dragging logs across stream channels or otherwise interfering with natural stream flow can materially affect the quality of water as well as affect the suitability of the stream as a home for fish.

## WOOD PRODUCTION

As with other aspects of forestry, we know more about the physical and biological possibilities of wood production than we do about the possibilities of any other output of the forest. But our knowledge here, as with many other aspects of forestry, is inadequate.

In a great many respects, wood production from forests today resembles crop agriculture thousands of years ago. Our ancient ancestors gathered the seeds, fruits, and nuts they could find, which grew "naturally." They may have scattered some seeds of grasses or cereals, probably unintentionally, and they may possibly have given some more or less haphazard protection to the growing plants against birds and animals which sought the same plant growth for their food. If ancient man exerted any change in the genetic stock of the crops on which he fed, it was inadvertent and poorly understood. Recent archaeological investigations have shown that "edible" in those days included food we would not consider edible today. Edible food (even by their standards) per unit area of land was very low, even under the most favorable conditions, but man's total numbers were correspondingly low, and in many areas he skirted famine much of the time.

The cultivated farm crops of today are vastly different from these ancient foods in all parts of the world. There has been massive deliberate genetic change in most crops, to the point where some, such as corn, could no longer survive without man's manipulation. The soil is cultivated in various ways, chemicals of various kinds are added to increase the capacity of the soil to feed the desired crops, and water is added or retained or drained off in some cases to produce more nearly optimum soil moisture conditions for the crops. The farmer usually seeks a form of monoculture, at least to the extent of trying to get rid of the "weeds" or unwanted plants that rob the desired plants of light, water, and fertility. He tries to control insects, plant diseases, and predators on his crops.

Many ecologists decry the monoculture and the intensive methods of much modern agriculture, but they are necessary to the continued existence of the 3½ billion people now living on earth and to the existence of the 6 to 7 billion people that will be living within a generation. The ancient food-gathering did not support more than half a billion people, if that many, and certainly could not support the population today or in the future. This is not to argue that modern agriculture is perfect or that no better way to produce food is possible; nor does it argue that wood production can or should follow exactly in the course of dŏmestic crop production.

For a long time in the United States, wood production and harvest was dominated by the immense natural stands of timber that the early colonists found here. The timber industry consisted largely of harvesting these natural stands of timber, more or less like our ancient ancestors harvested the seeds of wild grasses and grains. During the twentieth century, forestry as a profession has gradually been concerned not only with protection and management of the inherited timber stands, but with growing new volumes of timber. Each successive timber inventory of the Forest Service has shown an increase in wood growth, nationally. Even in the Pacific Northwest, where much of the remaining old growth timber is found, tree growth on previously cutover forest land is producing successively larger volumes of timber in the smaller sizes of trees—those grown since the larger old growth trees were cut on those lands.

Forestry of varying degrees of intensity is practiced on much forest land in the United States today. Intensive forestry, like intensive agriculture, may include many steps: preparation of the site for the new plants, choice of seeds or seedlings, cultural practices during the growth cycle, provision of plant nutrients to the growing plants, harvest at intervals, protection of the plants against their enemies, and other practices. Each of these measures has a physical effect upon wood growth, and their combined effect is often greater than the sum of their individual effects. For instance, it may do little or no good to fertilize a forest which is only lightly stocked, for there will be too few trees to take advantage of the increased plant food.

Intensified forestry for wood production depends upon the biological situation of each site, including the present stand of timber, and upon the goals of management. If there exists a substantial present stand of healthy growing timber, and the objective is to make periodic harvests (at intervals, say, of five years), then certain intensification measures would be appropriate. If the present stand is fully mature, making little or no net growth, with considerable rot due to past disease and insect attacks or with the high probability of heavy losses due to disease and insect attacks in the next few years, then a wholly different program of intensified forestry for wood production is appropriate. This book is not the place for a detailed discussion of these technical forestry matters, nor am I qualified to undertake such a discussion. But the physical and biological potentialities of intensified forestry for wood production are very great—much greater than most nonforesters realize.

One "scenario" for managing a forested area of the United States to produce the maximum wood output per acre annually—ignoring all cost considerations and all impacts on other uses and assuming adequate fire, disease, and insect control—might go as follows:

1. Harvest all the existing wild trees. For many forests, especially mature ones, there are many defective or low quality tree stems which are not worth taking out of the forest if economic considerations are dominant. For the mature stands, these defective stems are the result of fire, rot, disease, and insect damage, as well as of age. For many stands of second, third, or any cut, the existing stems are poor because the better ones have been removed in the form of selective cutting so often applied to such stands. Partly for aesthetic reasons, but partly also for future wood production, much if not all the defective wood must be removed from the forest, used if possible, and the rest piled and probably burnt on the ground. Control over logging and cleanup is obviously necessary. The objective is to leave a reasonably clean area for new forest planting.

2. Choose the tree species best adapted to the location, develop genetically superior planting stock, well-suited to the elevation, climate, soil, and other circumstances of the site, and have it ready for planting when needed. Wild trees are genetically highly mixed; trees interbreed to a degree most laymen do not realize. Many of the seedlings resulting from such crosses perish in the selection process which always takes place as some young trees crowd out others during the growing years. In wild strains of most species, there is a statistically normal distribution of ability to grow wood annually, ranging from very low to very high, with most trees in a middle range. If seed is selected from that fourth of the trees showing highest annual growth rates, the resulting seedlings will also have a normal distribution of growth rates but around a higher median. About four rounds of such selection will produce trees which can grow twice as fast, on the average, as the parent stock under the same growing conditions.

The geneticist regards selection among naturally occurring populations as a primitive form of genetic improvement for any species. It is only the first step along a pathway which may lead to wholly new plant forms, but for plant populations as diverse as the usual forest, selection can go a long way. Selection would somewhat narrow the range of genetic variability in a tree species but would by no means eliminate it altogether. Indeed, it would be very undesirable to eliminate all genetic variability in a tree species on a particular site, for that would leave the trees undesirably vulnerable to disease. Means have been found to test the small tree seedlings in the greenhouse or nursery before transplanting and to identify those which have the highest growth potential. Techniques are being developed to greatly reduce the age of sexual reproduction of trees and to permit vegetative reproduction from plant tissues. Forestry may well be on the brink of a genetic revolution.

3. Immediately plant the cleared and prepared site with the improved genetic stock; this might be seedlings of a single species or it might be seedlings of two or more desired species. Do not allow reproduction of wild stands of trees, if this can easily be prevented, or at least get the improved seedlings into the ground as early as natural seeding can possibly take place. Lose no time in getting a new stand growing; have as the objective, the successful planting of a logged site within a year after logging. Plant the seedlings at the proper spacing for rapid growth, including an allowance for some natural mortality.

4. On some sites it may be necessary to do some weeding as the young trees grow, to remove undesired trees or shrubs which have seeded naturally and which deprive the desired trees of light, moisture, or fertility. This weeding might be done by mechanical or chemical means, sometimes with larger machinery but often with a good deal of hand labor.

5. When this stand reaches an appropriate age and size, make a precommercial thinning. This will not produce any marketable material, and the cut material will remain in the forest. Carry out the thinning at the lowest possible cost. Expect that this thinning will usually have little effect upon wood production per acre, though sometimes it may increase it, but expect that such thinning will concentrate on fewer stems on such wood growth as does occur, thus making for larger trees at harvest date. Larger trees can often be used in ways that smaller trees cannot be used, and they can be harvested more economically than can an equal volume of wood in smaller trees.

6. At a later date—or later dates—make a commercial thinning, to remove some trees for poles or piling or as a source of pulpwood. This thinning may be expected to produce some net income, but, again, the chief gain from thinning will be a concentration of growth on fewer stems. To the extent necessary, each thinning should be used as a means of improving the spacing of the remaining trees to facilitate rapid and uniform growth.

7. Fertilize the forest at the appropriate stage or stages in its growth cycle. For most forests, this will be only nitrogen fertilizer at intervals of perhaps five years; the effect on growth should be considerable with little or no added nitrogen in the runoff.

8. Harvest the trees at the optimum age, which will depend upon species and site as well as age and perhaps upon the intended use of the wood. Some uses are basically related to wood volume, while others place a higher value on certain types of wood growth than upon others. The harvest might proceed in two or more stages in a shelterwood cut, or it might be completed in one clearcut, but the final cut should in any case remove all of the original trees. Harvest the site clean and remove not only all harvestable material but all other wood as well. A forest grown in this way can be expected to have a minimum of unusable wood, vastly less than the initial cut which started this rotation, and hence the aesthetic impact of harvest will be less.

9. Utilize the harvested wood fully in the physical sense and profitably in the economic sense by manufacturing those products of the highest value and by utilizing scraps, chips, and sawdust for paper production.

10. Repeat the process.

Lest there be any confusion about the meaning of the foregoing several paragraphs, let me repeat the major qualifications about it: (1) the management program sought to increase greatly, if not to maximize, annual wood growth per acre; all environmental impacts and all other uses of the forest were ignored; in practice, of course, such impacts and such uses would have to be considered and trade-offs between wood production and other forest outputs evaluated; (2) no consideration was given to the economic profitability of the measures described; in chapter 7, we shall see that intensive forestry for wood growing is likely to be economic on the more productive sites and less profitable, or not profitable at all, on the less productive sites; and (3) this is only one of several "scenarios" of intensive forest management that could be devised. Although many of the principles are the same, the specific management practices would vary from site to site, perhaps greatly so.

In terms of purely physical and biological considerations, intensive forestry for wood production differs considerably, depending upon whether it is applied to the harvest and other management of an existing stand, or whether it is designed to produce wood on a forest site from which the existing stand has been or soon will be harvested completely. Even more diverse than the physical-biological concerns are the economic and social policies for managing existing as contrasted to new stands, especially when sites of different productivity are considered; but this is a matter for later chapters.

Ignoring economic and other considerations, some comparisons based entirely upon physical-biological potentials are nevertheless interesting (table 12). The actual wood growth in 1970 was only half that possible on fully stocked natural stands, and that in turn was not much more than half of the growth possible under intensive forestry; these comparisons hold, in general, for the United States as a whole and for the Pacific Northwest Douglas fir region. The physical-biological potential exists for very great increases in annual wood growth in the United States. With such great physical-biological potential for wood growing, it should be possible to work out trade-offs between wood and other outputs of the forest, which would produce ample wood and also major forest outputs of other types.

SUSTAINED YIELD AND EVEN FLOW

Professional foresters have long been concerned with the future productivity of the forests they manage and with the employment and community stability which an assured and permanent supply of wood makes possible. European foresters developed and applied the concepts of sustained yield, managed forests, and related ideas long before there were American foresters. In a managed forest, the cut would equal the growth annually; young trees would be putting on new wood growth, while older trees would be harvested at some stage of maturity. The rotation might be by blocks or other acreage, or by clumps of trees within blocks; the harvest method might be clearcut, shelterwood cut, selective cut, or some other. The essential point is the purposeful management by the forester, with trees of different ages proceeding toward maturity and with the rate of harvest restricted to, but no lower than, the rate of growth so that the land is available for more growth.

The American forestry situation has always been very different from this concept of the managed forest. The Europeans who colonized North America inherited vast areas of forest, grown naturally with only the most limited intervention by man, mature and at the full volume of timber which a mature forest could sustain (except in those limited cases of recent natural fires or blowdowns). From the standpoint of managed forestry, this situation was as abnormal as a forested area completely denuded of trees would have been— each is at one end of a spectrum from cutover area to mature stand. From earliest colonial days until well into the twentieth century the timber industry was largely or wholly cutting mature old growth timber. During these many decades, forest land was being cleared for farming—in some cases, magnificent forests were cut and the trees burned where they fell to convert the land to cropping. For a long time, there was little or no concern about the future supply of wood, for two main reasons: the supply of wood seemed limitless, and the

Table 12.   Per Acre and Total Wood Production under Defined Physical (Biological)
Alternatives

| Region and alternative forest situation | Productive site classes included in calculation | Annual wood growth per acre in U.S. or in region (cu. ft.) | Total annual wood growth in U.S. or region (bill. cu. ft.) |
|---|---|---|---|
| United States as whole | | | |
| 1970 actual situation | all | 37 | 18 |
| Fully stocked natural stands | all | 75 | 37 |
| Intensive forestry [a] | all | 137 | 68 |
| Pacific Northwest Douglas fir [b] | | | |
| 1970 actual situation | all | 70 | 1.7 |
| Fully stocked natural stands[b] | I–III | 155 | 3.0 |
| Intensive forestry [a] | I–III | 238 | 4.6 |

[a] Estimated by present author.
[b] Marion Clawson and William F. Hyde, "Managing the Forests of the Coastal Pacific Northwest for Maximum Social Returns," paper presented at British Columbia Timber Policy Conference in Vancouver, B.C., April 1974.

land would be cleared for agriculture anyway. These were the decades of "cut out and get out."

It was revulsion against the more extreme forms and results of this policy which led Gifford Pinchot and other early foresters to emphasize continued timber production from a forest; this was basic to the famous directive to the Forest Service (which Pinchot claims he wrote) to manage the national forests "for the greatest good to the largest number of people for the long run." Later, this general objective was translated into "sustained yield," and this in time became an article of faith, not only for the Forest Service but for the forestry profession. The 1960 Multiple Use-Sustained Yield Act directed the national forests to be managed for sustained yield, which was defined as "the achievement and maintenance in perpetuity of a high level annual or periodic output of the various renewable resources of the national forests without impairment of the productivity of the land."

So stated, and in general terms, few persons would challenge or reject sustained yield. But what does it really mean in practice? When one comes down from broad principles to specific applications, problems begin to arise. Just how shall sustained yield be calculated in a specific situation? The nonforester is baffled to find the ramifications and complexities of that question, and to learn what enormous differences in results may flow from what he naively thinks are a few merely technical assumptions or procedures. The problems get especially difficult, as one works to convert a wholly mature forest into a managed one. Over what time period shall the conversion process be spread? For what area shall the balance between growth and cut be calculated, especially during this conversion period? Just how "conservative" shall the management be, that is, how much discount for unknowns, risk, and so forth shall be applied in calculating the sustained yield cut? In practice, many foresters have arrived at answers which they intended to be highly conservative—well below what might be, but was not certainly, possible. Calculations as to optimum timing of timber harvest seem to be an economic determination to economists, yet foresters have typically approached such calculations on a biological basis.

In practice, sustained yield has been interpreted to mean small variations in annual cut or cuts, which on the average for a five- or ten-year period did not deviate significantly from the long term average. This version of sustained yield has been more recently and more properly designated as "even flow." The President's Advisory Panel on Timber and the Environment defined sustained yield as "the yield that a forest produces continuously at a given intensity of management" and even flow as "the production from a national forest or other unit of land of the same amount of timber each year for an indefinite period of time." Sustained yield connotes maintenance of productive capacity indefinitely, but without commitment as to variations in harvest within a rotation; even flow is a more specialized version of sustained yield, where the requirement of an almost exactly equal annual harvest is added.

It is application of either of these ideas to mature old growth forests which produce the problems. Instead of the idealized managed forest of the forester, imagine an old growth forest, all the land of equal productive capacity, all completely stocked with old trees, all of which are 150 years old, all of which are ripe for cutting. An area equal to 1/150 of the whole area could be cut each year; if this area restocked naturally and the trees grew at the same rate that the old growth stand had grown during its growing years, then in 150 years the cutting cycle would be complete and the cutting could begin again on the first tract; the last trees cut on this rotation would be 300 years old—if they survived that long. By this time, this would be a managed forest on a 150-year rotation. Throughout that 150 year period, volume of timber cut each year would have exceeded volume of timber grown, although management would be fully on a "sustained yield" basis. Even the forester who places little emphasis on interest costs and economic returns may be repelled by such a long rotation, but many national forests where the mature trees averaged 150 or more years in age have been cut in the past on a rotation of 100 years or more.

If the area cut is exactly equal each year and if the stand is completely uniform, there is an even flow of wood volume cut each year during the first rotation. If the rotation is shortened to 100 years, and if trees grow at the same rate as did the mature trees during their growing years, there will necessarily be a drop in annual cut after the first rotation is completed. The rate of annual growth may be stepped up, in some of the ways suggested earlier in this chapter, so that in the second rotation of 100 years as much wood will be grown as previously was grown in 150 years; in this case, the annual cut after the first rotation need not drop off at all. The physical and biological possibilities of sustained yield and even flow do not in the least mean that either is the most economic use of the land and timber resource; that determination requires additional calculations.

In practice, of course, no area exactly conforms to this model any more than any forest exactly conforms to a model of managed forest. But some of the national forests were not so greatly different from this model; one may easily relax the specification of equal land productivity throughout the forest, and adjust area cut annually to vary with differences in site productivity, for instance. Today, when some forest has almost surely been cut and hopefully restocked with growing trees while some old growth remains, the situation is vastly more complicated. It is still more complicated when forests in different ownerships are considered. Shall sustained yield be calculated for the national forests only, or for the forests of all ownerships in a region or locality? For how large a region or locality should the calculations be made? Shall one include the productivity of all forests with young growing trees, or shall he insist that the young growth not be counted until the trees are minimally harvestable? One may well accept the maintenance of forest productive *capacity* as basic, but then how does one calculate sustained yield? Shall we abandon even flow as no longer essential? The way these questions are answered may have very great consequences, in terms of annual harvest volume, methods of forest management, costs and returns from the forest, and the like. We cannot, in this book, pursue these ideas in detail, but we warn the reader that innocent "good" words like "sustained yield" and "even flow" have immense and not always desirable ramifications and consequences.

## PHYSICAL AND BIOLOGICAL CONSEQUENCES

Thus far in this chapter we have been talking about the physical and biological feasibility of different practices and uses in forests.

But what are the consequences of any action within the forest? If the forest manager decides to cut a stand, in some manner or another, what are the physical and biological consequences of that decision, in terms of the kind of forest that will exist there five, ten, twenty, or fifty years from now? Or if he decides against any cut now, what are the future consequences of that decision? Or suppose that a decision is made to reserve an area from cutting as a wilderness, but to open it to uncontrolled wilderness use; what are the physical and biological consequences of that decision? Or suppose that a decision is made to control the extent of use of an established wilderness area; what are the consequences of that decision? Similar questions may be posed for every other forest use.

All such decisions have some common aspects. The decision—including the decision not to act—is taken now; the consequences come later and, for forests, often many years or some decades later. The actor in the decision process often does not bear the consequences of his action. This is particularly true in a public agency where men are moved from location to location, as in the Forest Service, but it is true for privately owned forests as well. Some of the consequences are not borne by the actor because they do not occur in the forest; this is especially true for actions which affect stream flow, for instance. The physical and biological consequences of many forest management decisions are unknown, at least to a degree. Some may be unpredictable, on the basis of our present knowledge—side effects if you will; and there is always a substantial component of risk and chance. If weather is favorable, one result may be obtained; if weather is unfavorable, quite a different result may occur.

The environmental impact statements required by the National Environmental Policy Act of 1970 are an attempt to measure the future physical impact of proposed actions. Such statements are designated as environmental impact statements, but this is probably a misnomer. They should more properly be called environmental impact projections, for they are always estimates of future impact of proposed present actions, and the actual impact may differ greatly from the projected one. In a great many cases, even well informed specialists cannot be sure what the physical and biological consequences of some action will be. Who bears the consequences, if some projections do not actually work out in practice? There has been a rather long history of cost–benefit analysis, especially as applied to federal water development programs. In general, the calculations of estimated costs and benefits have not proven accurate—costs have typically been higher than estimated, and benefits have typically been lower. In the case of public programs, neither the cost calculator nor the immediate beneficiary of the program is required to bear the consequences of these miscalculations; those costs fall upon the general taxpayer. Similarly, if a public agency forester decides to pursue an extremely conservative program of harvesting mature old growth timber, this forester does not bear the costs of his decision; they, too, fall upon the general taxpayer or the consumer.

# 7.

## Economic Efficiency in Forestry

Merely because it is physically and biologically possible to produce some output from a forest or to make some use of it, does not prove that it is economically efficient to do so. Economic efficiency is one of the tests or considerations in forest policy noted in chapter 3. Here we shall be concerned only with the question of the total value of the outputs in relation to the total cost of the inputs—measuring values and costs without regard to their distribution among persons. In chapter 8 we shall briefly consider the next question: who gets the benefits and who pays the costs?

Economic efficiency requires the greatest output of desired goods and services from a given amount of inputs, or a designated quantity and kind of output for the least cost of those inputs whose costs must be considered. In less formal language, it requires the greatest returns per dollar spent or invested in forest management. An economically optimum production plan or policy produces a more favorable relationship between desired outputs and measured inputs than can any alternative production plan or policy, or than can be secured from the same or similar inputs used in any other way. The absolute difference between value of outputs and cost of inputs should be maximized, not the ratio between them (as in the typical benefit–cost ratio).

One basic problem in application of economic standards is to define what outputs are desired. This depends upon the forest owner's objectives or goals. If his goal is money income, then clearly it is net money income which is to be maximized, but if his objective is some sort of personal or psychic return, then maximization of this output may or may not maximize money return. Later in this chapter, we get into the question of forest owners' objectives.

Another basic problem is the measurement of outputs from the plan or policy that were not sought by the forest owner or that do not accrue to him, and of costs of production that he does not pay. For instance, a certain type of forest management might be undertaken to produce wood for money income but might also have repercussions upon stream flow, wildlife, and other aspects or outputs of the forest. The forest owner would be unable to capture the positive values so created, if any, and he might evade any losses he may have caused to others. The economically efficient plan and program for him, from his point of view, might therefore differ considerably from the economically efficient plan and program for all persons with an interest in the forest. This is the divergence between individual and social viewpoints which so often arises in natural resource management.

Partly because the interval between initiation of a forestry plan or management program and the realization of its results is often very long—measured perhaps in decades, not merely in years—the way that time is taken into account in forest economic efficiency studies is extremely important. The usual way to include time is by use of the interest rate—an interest charge upon invested capital or upon capital which could be released by some other plan or program of management—or by the calculation of an internal rate of return from the forestry operation. But such a statement largely evades the real issue: How high should the interest rate used for such calculations be? For many forestry programs, the choice of the interest rate will affect the result more than any other single step—at 3 percent, many programs are profitable, while at 8 percent many of these will drop by the wayside. But use of interest charges, while basic, may not be adequate for handling time considerations in some forestry situations. Some private owners are unwilling to consider returns beyond some relatively short period, irrespective of the interest rate that could be earned, and some persons have argued that society should take an indefinitely long view of its forest management, again largely irrespective of interest rate.

Partly because of the long time involved in fruition of many forestry programs, and partly because of climatic and other variables, planning for future forestry is inevitably uncertain. For a public agency or for a private owner operating over a very large area, these uncertainties may or may not average out. In the past, certain trends in forest product prices have been pronounced; in general, lumber prices (measured in dollars with constant purchasing power) have risen at an average (cumulative) rate of about 1.8 percent annually since about 1800, while for the past thirty or fifty years there has been only a slight rise or no rise at all (in constant dollars) for plywood and pulpwood. Can these trends of the past be safely projected into the future? If so, they significantly affect the prospects for growing sawlogs.

Planning an economically optimum output from a forest requires both physical substitution curves; i.e., how much output of one use is affected by increases in another use, and production functions or physical input-output curves; i.e., if a certain amount of fertilizer is applied in a given forest situation, how much does wood growth respond? Such curves are likely to be needed for forest planning for combinations or volumes of uses, or for kinds or volumes of inputs that are different than have been experienced in the past.

As one contemplates the application of economic analysis and the use of the test of economic efficiency for publicly owned forests, the question immediately arises: How far are we willing to abide by the results of such tests? The enthusiasm of forest users for economic analysis applied to a publicly owned forest seems to be highly correlated with their expectation of the results of such analysis. If a group thinks economic analysis will show its desired use of the forest as the economically most valuable, then it is likely to support such analysis more enthusiastically than if it suspects that some other use will produce a higher net economic return.

APPLICATION OF ECONOMICS TO FORESTS

Economic analysis can be applied to all the forest outputs described in tables 1 and 2 of chapter 4. In theory, exactly the same kinds of data on amounts and costs of inputs into the production process, of quantities and values of outputs from that process, and of the relationship between output and input at each scale of operation or each intensity of operation, are needed and are sufficient. In practice, serious difficulties arise. It is very hard to place a value on some kinds of outputs. For example, nearly everyone will agree that wildlife has some value, but how much? Equally as serious as the conceptual problems (which may always persist) are the present severe deficiencies of data for both inputs and outputs of some of the forest uses other than wood production.

Thus, in practice, economics of forestry is likely to come down to economics of growing wood. As in so many other places in this book, I would like to discuss each forest output in more or less the same terms but wind up talking about wood production because so much more (but still inadequate) data are available for it than for any other forest output. There is another and perhaps more defensible reason for focusing on wood production: although the motivation for growing wood is not invariably profit or economic return from the wood, yet the profit motive or the economic calculation is more likely to be applied to wood production than to any other forest output.

When wood is considered, a basic distinction must be made between the harvesting of whatever volume of wood a tract now possesses and the growing of a new wood supply on that tract. In a sense, the willingness of the forest owner to harvest and his willingness to grow wood are each a form of supply, in the economist's sense of that term. There is often a large time difference between them—harvest of standing stock can take place immediately, but growing of new trees takes years, even decades. But a more important economic distinction between these kinds of supply is the difference between willingness to harvest and sell wood out of stock or inventory and willingness to invest new capital to produce new inventory. The situation is similar to that of a storekeeper who is faced with selling an inventory he now possesses, perhaps one he inherited, but who must consider buying new inventory if he is to stay in business.

As a matter of fact, this difference between harvesting existing timber stands and growing new stands is quantitatively very important in the United States. Substantial volumes of old growth timber still exist, especially on public forests, and considerable volumes of regrowth, much of which arose "naturally" and without conscious investment or management effort by the owner, also exist on private forests. The economics of harvesting these stands is very different from the economics of growing new stands on these same forest lands. The difference between harvesting and growing is especially acute on the less productive forest sites.

We have calculated that wood can be profitably grown, both by good "natural" forestry (the reasonably good management of natural stands of timber) and by highly intensive forestry, on productive site classes I through III and sometimes on site class IV lands, in the Pacific Northwest Douglas fir region and in the Southern pine region.[1] An interest rate of 6 percent was used to calculate the costs incurred in stand establishment and management over the years until the harvest occurred. On these lands, the costs of growing wood, including the extra costs of growing additional wood by more intensive management, are substantially less than the probable future selling price of the wood when it is harvested. For each of these regions, the costs of wood growing on site class V and on much of site class IV exceeded the value of the wood that could be produced. In these calculations, it was necessary to use the Forest Service classification of site productivity (which is based on purely physical factors, as we

[1] Marion Clawson, "Conflicts, Strategies, and Possibilities for Consensus in Forest Land Use and Management," *Forest Policy for the Future*, LW Working Paper No. 1 (Washington: Resources for the Future, Inc., 1974).

noted earlier); an economic classification of sites would have been preferable, but the general principle is sound. Many investment and management costs are as high per acre on poor as on good sites, and some may be higher; annual output of wood is substantially less, sometimes less than a fourth as much. An economically rational man, company, or public agency would incur no expenses for growing timber on these less productive sites—although he might incur expenses of forest management for other purposes. Left alone, they might grow some timber after harvest, but he would be ill-advised to spend any money to produce wood on such sites.

The economics of harvesting an inherited or existing volume of timber on a site is very different. If one considers only the economics of wood supply, then the costs of harvesting the timber, including the cost of building needed roads, must be compared with the value of the wood so harvested. Timber volume per acre and timber quality are generally lower on the less productive than on the more productive sites. In addition, the less productive sites may be rougher land and—at least sometimes—more remote from good public roads. Hence, neither value of timber nor cost of harvest is necessarily the same on poor as on good sites. If the value of the wood is greater than the cost of getting it out, then harvest is "economic" or at least profitable in this narrow sense; it may mean only that the owner is converting the capital tied up in standing timber into cash or readily investable capital. A private owner can scarcely be expected not to harvest existing timber stands under these conditions, if he is interested only in monetary return. The present income from harvesting the standing timber on many low-quality forest sites is greater than the present value of the discounted stream of income from future wood production, even if the latter be estimated forever into the future. If the forest is publicly owned, the same comparisons of present and future value of wood are valid, but the public agency might well decide to forego harvest of the timber because of other values of the forest, such as recreation or wildlife, which the private owner is often unable to capture. The public agency and indeed some private owners, especially the smaller ones, may have objectives other than money income maximization and hence may decide not to harvest existing stands of timber.

The difference in economic productivity of different forest sites for the growing of wood can be approached from another direction—the rate of return which can be earned from different forest management practices as applied to different forest types and site classes under different assumptions as to future wood prices. The rate of return from forest plantings varies from 2½ to 9 percent annually, depending upon species and location, site class of the forest, and price assumption for the timber grown (table 13). It is notable that site class affects returns more than do timber price or species and location. The returns from stand improvement (the pre-commercial type of thinning discussed in chapter 6) are substantially higher than for tree planting—roughly double—and again site class is more important than either timber price or species and location. A package of forestry practices, and consideration of the possibility that wood prices may advance so that gains are made from higher prices for standing as well as for newly grown timber, still further increases the prospective rates of return. While site class is still more important than species and location, the extent of price rises during the period of timber growth has a more important influence on returns to management than on returns to plantings or stand improvement alone.

Two other economic considerations must be introduced, though briefly. Each has many complex ramifications about which much debate can be and has been stirred up, and which can be presented here only in the simplest terms. All of the foregoing discussion about economics of wood growing and of investment for this purpose has been in terms of a generally constant price level for commodities as a whole; wood prices, and more particularly lumber prices, are assumed to rise in relation to that general price level, as they have in the past. But no general inflation of prices has been introduced. If a general inflation continues more or less indefinitely into the future in the United States, then wood prices, stumpage prices (standing trees in the forest), and forest land prices will almost surely rise in terms of current dollars. This might seem to argue for purchase of forest land and standing timber as a hedge against inflation, but this type of forest and timber purchase seems not to have been widespread, at least up to now. However, one cannot be sure, because many purchases of forest land, nominally as a hobby or for personal recreation, may in fact have had substantial anti-inflation motivation. But purchase of forest land and timber as a hedge against inflation should be compared with, or evaluated against, other kinds of anti-inflationary precautionary measures; the low liquidity of investment in forests, at least in some areas, should be considered carefully. Shortly after the beginning of the twentieth century, many persons of wealth were led to purchase forest land and timber on the basis that a "timber famine" was coming, and by and large such investments were unprofitable. Forests, as indeed all other kinds of property, may be good investments in some situations for some people, but they are not magic sources of wealth in every location for every investor.

Another economic consideration is what is commonly called "the

Table 13. Rates of Return to Given Investments in Forest Improvement under Various Price Assumptions, by Type and Site Class of Forest (percentage rates of return)

| Forest type and site class [a] | Type of investment and softwood lumber price index (1967 = 100) | | | | | | | | | | | |
|---|---|---|---|---|---|---|---|---|---|---|---|---|
| | Forestation [b] | | | | Sapling stand improvement | | | | Management intensification | | | |
| | Price index at harvest: | | | | Price index at harvest: | | | | Price change during rotation: | | | |
| | 115 | 144 | 180 | 225 | 115 | 144 | 180 | 225 | None | 115–144 | 115–180 | 115–122 |
| Hemlock-spruce | | | | | | | | | | | | |
| I or II | 5.8 | 6.6 | 7.5 | 8.4 | 10.2 | 11.5 | 12.2 | 14.1 | 14.4 | 18.0 | 23.5 | 31.7 |
| III | 3.8 | 4.6 | 5.2 | 5.6 | 6.7 | 7.7 | 8.7 | 9.7 | 7.0 | 8.8 | 11.3 | 15.3 |
| IV | 3.0 | 3.6 | 4.2 | 4.8 | 5.2 | 6.0 | 6.8 | 7.6 | 5.0 | 6.3 | 8.1 | 10.9 |
| Douglas fir and fir-spruce | | | | | | | | | | | | |
| I or II | 6.0 | 6.9 | 7.7 | 8.6 | 10.6 | 11.3 | 13.2 | 14.5 | 16.2 | 20.3 | 26.3 | 35.5 |
| III | 4.4 | 5.1 | 5.8 | 6.5 | 7.5 | 8.5 | 9.4 | 10.4 | 9.6 | 12.0 | 15.6 | 21.0 |
| IV | 3.4 | 4.0 | 4.6 | 5.2 | 5.7 | 6.5 | 7.3 | 8.1 | 6.4 | 8.0 | 10.4 | 14.0 |
| Ponderosa and lodgepole pines | | | | | | | | | | | | |
| I or II | 4.8 | 5.6 | 6.5 | 7.4 | 9.0 | 10.3 | 11.6 | 12.9 | 9.0 | 11.2 | 14.7 | 19.8 |
| III | 3.4 | 4.1 | 4.8 | 5.5 | 6.2 | 7.2 | 8.1 | 9.1 | 5.5 | 6.9 | 8.9 | 12.0 |
| IV | 2.5 | 3.1 | 3.7 | 4.3 | 4.5 | 5.3 | 6.0 | 6.8 | 3.5 | 4.4 | 5.7 | 7.6 |
| Southern, red, and white pines | | | | | | | | | | | | |
| I or II | 6.5 | 7.4 | 8.2 | 9.1 | 11.6 | 12.9 | 14.2 | 15.6 | 18.0 | 22.6 | 29.2 | 39.4 |
| III | 4.8 | 5.5 | 6.2 | 6.9 | 7.7 | 8.7 | 9.7 | 10.6 | 10.4 | 13.0 | 16.9 | 22.7 |
| IV | 3.7 | 4.3 | 5.0 | 5.6 | 6.1 | 6.9 | 7.7 | 8.5 | 7.2 | 9.0 | 11.7 | 15.7 |

Source: President's Advisory Panel on Timber and the Environment, Report of the President's Advisory Panel on Timber and the Environment (1973), p. 146.

[a] Site classes I and II include those forests capable of producing 120 cubic feet or more of timber per acre per year; site class III includes those producing 85–120 cubic feet; site class IV includes those producing 50–85 cubic feet.

[b] For derivation of these figures, see original source.

sustained yield effect." All of the foregoing economic calculations are based on growing costs and harvest values from the particular site. In some cases, the consequences of a forestry program on one site may be very great for the economics of wood growing and harvest on other sites. For instance, the national forests have a large volume of old growth timber, making little or no net growth annually. These lands are committed to sustained yield management, and the rate of harvest is governed, among other things, by the estimated time and rate of growth of timber after the present old growth volume has been harvested. If new and intensified management programs are begun on recently harvested sites, or on sites incompletely stocked and hence relatively unproductive, this affects greatly the estimates of future annual wood growth, and this can be translated into a higher rate of harvest of existing stands. This sustained yield effect is valid only where large volumes of old timber exist, where the owner (manager) is committed to a continued harvest of timber at rates not too greatly different from the present, and where some forest lands are producing significantly below their potential. These may seem, and indeed are, rather restrictive conditions, but they apply to a substantial proportion of the national forest commercial timber area today. Under these circumstances, an investment today to increase future timber volume can be translated into an increased harvest of timber today, not waiting for the years or decades until the trees planted today are mature, and this in turn makes such investment very much more profitable than it would otherwise be.

ECONOMICS OF FOREST INDUSTRY FORESTRY

A wood processing firm that owns a forest is presumably interested in maximizing its monetary profits from such forest ownership and management. Its objective is thus both simpler, more direct, and more easily stated than are the objectives of some other types of forest owners. But this apparently simple objective contains some complications. For how long a time period should income be maximized —perpetually, or as far ahead as one can reasonably think about the future, or for one rotation period of forest growing and harvest, or for the next decade, or for some other period? Since a forest industry forest is, by definition, part of a firm that has wood processing facilities, there is the possibility that the economically optimum program for timber growing will not be the same as the economically optimum program for wood processing; if so, which dominates, or is it the combined program which is dominant?

Most forest industry firms face a reasonably competitive market for the lumber, plywood, paper, or other products they produce. Some may produce primarily for a local market, while others produce for a regional or national one, but in nearly all cases a single firm has such a small share of the relevant market that it is, economically speaking, a competitive market.

A forest industry firm is generally unable to capture the values other than wood production which arise out of its forest management. Most forest industry firms get little or no monetary income from the outdoor recreation which takes place on their lands. Only in rare cases is there any real prospect of profit from provision of outdoor recreation opportunity, in part because publicly owned parks and forests provide similar recreation opportunity free or at prices far below cost. Usually forest industry firms would be better off, economically, if they could somehow exclude the public from outdoor recreation on their forests, but in many cases it would be physically impossible, or very difficult, to do this, and the public relations or "image" created by such efforts would often be disadvantageous to the firm. On the whole, the forest industry has been most generous to the public, not only making its forests available for such extensive recreation as hunting, berry picking, and other activities, but positively assisting users in such activities, and in many cases providing them with picnic areas or campgrounds free or at costs to the user that are well below costs to the firm. This may have paid off to the forest industry firms in terms of a more favorable political and economic climate.

Forest industry firms are likewise unable to collect for the value of the wildlife which grows in their forests or for special programs to enhance wildlife values; likewise, they are unable to collect for water originating on their lands or for programs to preserve or to enhance the water values. In their economic calculus, these firms must ignore such wildlife and water values except to the extent that they are required by law to consider them or to the extent they do so as part of overall programs of public relations. Forest industry firms cannot possibly provide wilderness areas on their lands, for wilderness is directly in conflict with wood production.

Forest industry firms that buy wood from public or private forests in addition to wood grown on their own lands, often face something less than fully competitive markets in the economic sense of the term. There are likely to be only a few other possible competitors in the local supply area, and the actions of each firm are thus taken into account by the others. In bidding for national forest timber, for instance, one firm is likely to take the probable bidding of rival firms into account, resulting in intensive and sometimes highly personal competition, or it may tacitly accept the other firm, an accommodation which avoids direct conflict. In this situation, the Forest Service is often the chief, if not the only seller of timber; the competitive market of many sellers is absent. When a forest industry firm is buying wood from private suppliers, it may be loath to upset the established market by bidding more for wood, even temporarily, because paying more for an added supply quickly gets translated into the same higher price for its total purchased supply. In these cases, the firm may be economically well advised to grow its needed additional wood supply, even at costs for the marginal supply that are higher than the price it is paying for the purchased supply. In recent years a significant volume of southern pine of sawlog sizes has been used for pulp in spite of the fact that a customary analysis would show that the lumber outturn from a log was worth more than its pulp value. I interpret this situation to mean that paper companies are using their own sawlogs for pulp to avoid disturbing the market for the pulpwood they buy.

Several factors affect the willingness of a forest industry timber owner to harvest his present stand or volume of timber. One obvious factor is the rate at which standing trees will grow over the next few decades; if they are mature or old, with slow net growth rate, then the prospects for their growth are poorer than if they are in the thrifty fast-growing years. Another factor is his expectation of future wood product prices; if the trend seems upward, then he is in less of a hurry to sell than if the trend may be downward—in the latter case, he processes and sells as fast as possible. Current and prospective interest rates are also a factor; if they are high, then the holding cost of marketable timber is greater than if they are low. Real estate taxes are also a force pushing toward earlier harvest. His need for wood, to keep his processing plant operating at desired rate, is another factor. Other factors may influence particular timber processors or be important in particular situations, but these considerations are likely to be in the mind of any timber industry forest owner.

When it comes to growing timber by new plantings after a timber harvest or by purchase of land on which to establish a forest, the forest industry owner is influenced by some of the same factors, but for different time periods and perhaps in different ways. Now, his concern is with how fast wood will grow for the life cycle of the new stand; site class looms most important, and present stand—assuming he is making a new planting—is not a factor. Price outlook is still important, but now his reaction to prospective favorable prices is to grow more wood, not to hold back some for later harvest. The interest rate is still highly important because of the long time between planting and harvest; low interest rates help to make wood growing profitable while high interest rates make wood production uneconomic. The long-run need for wood for processing is still a factor, but trees planted now are likely to be processed in a plant not yet built; the present processing plant is likely to be fully depreciated and replaced before the newly planted trees reach marketable age. While the timber industry forest owner has more options before he plants a new stand than he has with an older stand, once the trees are planted and growth is well under way, his options shrink greatly.

Taxes are an important cost of timber growing, and the willingness of forest industry firms to grow timber depends in part upon their tax outlook. Some states have yield or severance taxes for forest products; part of the tax is paid when the timber is harvested, not annually as a real estate tax. While this is often praised as an important measure to encourage forestry, it is not found in all states and seems to have rather limited effect where it is optional. Timber growing is subject to capital gains taxation, rather than ordinary income tax rates in the federal income tax laws; this is a material advantage to the larger and more profitable firms.

Forest industry firms that own and operate forests certainly have problems—What productive enterprise does not?—and some firms surely fall short of average practice in the industry, and more fall short of best practice. Yet, with all these qualifications, the forest industry forests are operated more nearly for economic efficiency in wood growing than are the forests of any other major ownership class. It is no accident that the better managed forests of such firms in many ways practice the best timber management now to be found in the United States. Economic pressures are strong incentives for best performance, whether in forestry or elsewhere.

## ECONOMICS OF SMALL PRIVATE FORESTS

Most small private forest owners face a very different economic situation than the forest industry forest owner. For most of them, the objectives are different, in that most small owners do not expect to make a profitable return from the growing and sale of wood. Some of them are farmers; their woodlots are parts of their farms where the land will grow trees but not cultivated crops. Others may own the forest for their personal recreation, or as a hobby, or they may have inherited it, or they may own it hoping for increases in land value, or for various reasons other than for profit out of current wood production. Such owners presumably seek to maximize something from their forest ownership—their personal satisfactions, perhaps. For them, as for the forest industry owners, the question of the time period over which the maximization is to occur is important and may be critical. Such information as is available suggests that most such owners have a fairly short time horizon, often a few years, sometimes the remainder of their lifetimes, but rarely a full cycle or longer of tree planting, growth, and harvest.

The small private forest owner has many economic as well as technical difficulties on the production side of his forestry. The average "other private" owner has perhaps 150 acres of forest and of course many are smaller than average; even a minimum set of forest machinery and a minimum work crew will require 2,000 acres for reasonably full utilization. The farmer who owns a woodlot or the other small private forest owner who has other business activities and perhaps some machinery may be able to operate small forests effectively, but the alternative enterprise may reward his labor better than will the forest. Many small forest owners must hire firms or workers for such tasks as tree planting, thinning, and the like, but it may not be easy to find contractors or workers interested in relatively small jobs. If the small forest owner seeks to manage his forest carefully and intensively, he finds he must spend a lot of time learning the latest and best techniques, and the time actually spent in management of his forest may pay him relatively little. As a result, most small private forest owners neglect or ignore their forests, letting public agencies fight fires if they occur, perhaps keeping trespassers out, but mostly letting nature take its course in tree reproduction and growth.

The small private forest owner often faces difficulty in marketing the wood which does grow on his land to the best advantage. Partly because his land area is relatively small and hence the total volume of wood that may be harvested annually is small also, he is likely to make a sale of trees or stumpage at irregular and often long intervals. His need for cash may be more decisive than forestry considerations of optimum harvest date. In many cases, he will respond to the approaches of some woodbuyer, often a small sawmill owner, rather than deciding himself, for silvicultural or economic reasons, that a timber harvest is the most economic thing to do at some particular date. Frequently he sells all merchantable trees for a lump sum payment, and the buyer takes every tree that he thinks will repay the cost of manufacturing products from it without regard for the effect of such harvest upon the productive capacity of the remaining forest. The small forest owner often decides on such sales without getting bids from other possible purchasers, and, as a result, in most cases he does not receive the full value of the wood cut. In still other situations, the small private forest owner will find it difficult to sell his timber at all; he may have the low quality hardwoods described earlier, or he may be in an area where there are few processing facilities, or there may be a larger local supply of timber than there is market to absorb it so that buyers will be unenthusiastic about his timber.

Though the small private forest owner faces severe difficulties in both the production and the marketing aspects of his operations, yet the vast number and total area of such forests do result in a lot of wood being grown every year, and harvests, while irregular on each forest, total up to a lot of wood reaching the consumer each year. It is often said that the typical small private forest owner does a poor job of forestry. In the technical sense this is true, and in the economic sense this forest owner often gets less than a full return from his resource. But it is also true that this small forest owner often does a good forestry job, considering the handicaps under which he must operate. He may get little income from his forest, but he spends little money on it too. His short time horizon often keeps his stocking too low for optimum results, but he avoids the error of excessive stocking.

Perhaps a more important question than the economic returns from wood production is, To what extent does this small private forest owner gain his own objectives for his forest? If he owns it for his personal recreation, does it provide him with the greatest satisfactions at the least cost? If he owns the land for speculative gain in land prices, does he buy and sell the land at optimum times and at the best possible prices? Does he gain from the wildlife on his forest, in ways that he seeks? If one knew more precisely the objectives of any small private forest owner, then one could better judge how good a job he was doing in his forest management and better advise him how to attain more of the outputs he seeks.

The small private forest owner is in an even poorer position than the forest industry forest owner to secure an economic return from his land for the wildlife, water, and recreation for others which it produces or might produce. His position is worse in that he would usually find it more difficult to protect his land against trespass and to market the small volumes of these outputs than does the larger timber industry forest owner—and, as we saw earlier, the latter has major problems in this regard.

Is there a public interest in aiding—subsidizing—these small private forest owners? In the past and at present, some forms of public assistance have been and are available to them, and proposals have been made to increase the scope and amount of such public help. It is argued that the area of small private forests is so large, the potential productive capacity is so great, and the present output is so far below potential that there would be a substantial public gain in the form of larger wood supplies, if these forests were managed more intensively. According to the Forest Service data presented in table 5, the relationship between actual growth and potential growth on the average small private forest was exactly the same as the average for all forests—lower than for forest industry forests, higher than for national forests. Admittedly, performance might be much higher, but compared with other forests it is not bad. Past programs to help small private forest owners have not generated much enthusiasm among such owners and have not been highly successful in terms of total additional wood produced, although some have argued that this is because the scale of such public programs has been too small.

If there is a public interest in increased wood production from these small private forests, might a different approach in the future be more successful than the provision of technical assistance, planting stock, and similar public programs have been in the past? Might there be some way in which the owner could retain the land for his desired use, such as recreation, yet put its management for wood production in the hands of some person or group with more technical skill and greater ability to manage forests and sell their output effectively? One such proposal has been for public aid to timber management organizations—private forest consultants, land management companies, cooperatives, units of local government, and others—which would lease the timber growing capacity from the small owner, conduct planned forestry operations on a substantial proportion of all forest land within a local area, sell the output on the best terms, and share the income from wood production. There would undoubtedly be many difficulties in working out equitable arrangements, but this approach might provide for greater wood production and more financial returns to the forest owner, especially in some situations. Perhaps special tax concessions or special subsidies could be extended to any small private forest owner who would put the management of his lands in the hands of a licensed professional forester. Would it be desirable to try these and other approaches—perhaps on an experimental basis?

Whatever the forms of public assistance extended to small private forest owners, how far should technical and economic criteria determine to whom such assistance is extended, and how far should the assistance be available to any small private forest owner who seeks it? Such public assistance would surely produce more wood per dollar expended if limited to site classes I, II, and III than if extended to poorer site classes; if limited to areas, forest types, tree species, and other attributes of the forest where the market for additional wood is best; and if limited to forests above some minimum size, say 100 (or even 300) acres. But it may be argued that every small private forest owner, no matter what the size of his forest, no matter what its site quality, and no matter what kind of wood he could produce, is entitled to public help if he desires it.

## THE ECONOMICS OF NATIONAL FOREST ADMINISTRATION

The Forest Service, as the agency charged with the administration of the national forests, faces a very different set of economic problems than either the forest industry or small private forest owners. The objectives of national forest administration are stated in the Multiple Use-Sustained Yield Act of 1960 as (in part) ". . . the management of all the variable renewable surface resources of the national forests so that they are utilized in the combination that will best meet the needs of the American people . . . harmonious and coordinated management of the various resources, each with the other, without impairment of the productivity of the land, with consideration being given to the relative values of the various resources, and not necessarily the combination of uses that will give the greatest dollar return or the greatest unit output."

This general, somewhat imprecise, and even somewhat contradictory language may be described as suggesting some economic efficiency—but not too much—in national forest administration. "Best meets the needs of the American people" surely might be interpreted as achieving the greatest economic efficiency, or the most output per unit of input and presumably for all forest outputs in combination; so might the phrase "relative values of the resources"; but "greatest dollar return" is specifically rejected as the single or dominant goal though it might, under some circumstances, be one goal. The same Act directs the management of the national forests for sustained yield of the various outputs of the forests; on some of the less productive sites, this type of management for timber would produce a lower present value of output than would an immediate and complete harvesting of all merchantable timber and a subsequent neglect of the forest site.

The 1960 Act originated in the Forest Service and was fully acceptable to its top personnel. Perhaps more important than the wording of the Act—which could be interpreted in different ways—have been the attitudes of foresters in general and of Forest Service foresters in particular. Emphasis has generally been put upon "conservation," "multiple use," "sustained yield," "good silvicultural practice," ecological considerations, and the like. Maximization of economic returns, to the extent that, or wherever, this differed from these resource management criteria, has been of lesser importance or of no importance at all as a management criterion.

Economic management of the national forests would, in any case, be more difficult than economic management of large private forests. The latter can use market prices as a guide to their economic decisions in a way that the Forest Service cannot. With half of all the softwood sawtimber on national forests—and a much higher proportion in some regions—the market for softwood sawlogs and products made from them is, to a very large extent, what the Forest Service makes it. In any line of economic activity, one firm which has half the resources or half the total output cannot operate as if its actions did not affect the market. On the contrary, its direct and indirect effects are very great, whether it acknowledges its influence or tries to pretend it does not exist. If the Forest Service were to offer substantially more or substantially less stumpage for sale, this would affect the price of all stumpage and of all lumber, and this in turn would affect the willingness of private firms to grow and to market timber. Similarly, if the Forest Service were to price outdoor recreation on national forests at several times the present level, this would affect the numbers of people who visit national forests and also affect the ability and willingness of private forest owners to provide outdoor recreation.

Economic management of the national forests is also difficult because of the nature of the federal appropriation process. The Multiple Use Act of 1960 might seem to require the calculation of economic values of the various outputs or uses of the national forests and a comparison of the value of one use with another. However, this has never been done in information available to the public, in the agency presentations to the Office of Management and Budget (OMB), in OMB's review of budget requests, or in the Congressional appropriation process. There is little or no evaluation of the effect of increased (or decreased) expenditures upon the values that could be created by the various uses of the forests. There is no capital account, and thus there is no charge for use of past investments or for interest on current value of the timber stands. The budgeting-appropriation process is too slow, starts too far ahead of the time period to which the budget is applicable, and relies too much on "last year." It makes really efficient management of the national forests difficult if not impossible. Although the national forests are big business in the modern American sense of the term, they have not been managed to any major degree as large economic enterprises. In the budget and appropriation process, appropriations for national forest management have been treated essentially like social service expenditures of government, not like resource management outlays from which economic returns are expected.

Economic management of the national forests is further complicated by the fact that many of the outputs of these forests produce little or no cash income. As we have noted in earlier chapters, a forest output may have economic as well as social value even when no payment is made for it, or when the payment is arbitrarily low, but there is always a problem of estimating the economic value of such outputs. Pricing them at or near zero certainly encourages their use and exaggerates their social value. Outdoor recreation and wilderness use of national forests are at least two instances in which low costs or minimal charges to the users have encouraged heavy, not to say excessive, use.

Although measurement of the economic value of some of the national forest outputs is difficult, some progress has been made in such measurement in recent years. Even if the value of such outputs could be measured with tolerable accuracy, how should use charges be based? Should they be at the level which would maximize revenue from such uses, or at a level where all the costs of providing such services were met? Either of these two criteria would result in charges for outdoor recreation, wilderness use, stream flows, and some other outputs of the national forest very much higher than the current low charges for these uses.

There are still other problems in managing national forests for maximum economic output. In some local markets, the Forest Service has great difficulty in getting the full economic value for the stumpage which it sells. Many local markets are far from competitive in the economist's sense of the term, and prices bid are often at the level of the Forest Service appraisal of the timber; in other markets, where competition is more active, prices bid may be much higher. A more important inefficiency, from the national viewpoint, is that the wood production on national forests is not closely integrated in any technical or economic sense with the industries that process the wood. The Forest Service can merely offer stumpage for sale; only rarely can it specify how, or even where, this timber shall be manufactured, or into what products it is to be processed. While it may be assumed that most purchasers of national forest timber will seek the greatest economic value from that timber, yet their inability to plan on acquiring national forest timber year after year may make it impossible for them to secure the greatest value. The close integration of woods and mill which some of the largest private timber industry firms are able to achieve is lacking. If national forest timber is sold competitively, and is thus open to any purchaser, some inefficiency between growing and processing may be an inevitable price.

An economist judges or suspects two further major inefficiencies in national forest management: (1) timber inventories are excessive, and (2) annual management costs are excessive.

The optimum inventory of growing stock on national forests might be calculated in either of two ways: by comparison with inventories on forest industry forests of the same forest type, and by comparisons with intensively managed forests. Forests may be managed to produce the greatest output of wood per acre, which means cutting at the age of greatest mean annual wood growth per acre, or they may be managed to produce wood most economically, which means cutting trees at financial rather than at biological maturity. Since wood growth requires an existing stand of timber, and since such a stand has a value which can be realized by harvest, an interest allowance on the amount of capital which could be released by timber harvest is a proper cost of timber growing. Financial maturity thus always means harvesting trees at younger ages than does biological maturity, and it also means a lower investment in growing stock in relation to annual growth.

If the per acre average sawtimber stocking of national forests were reduced to the average per acre sawtimber stocking of forest industry forests, some 400 billion board feet or 40 percent of national sawtimber inventory could be released.[2] If we make the (possibly heroic) assumption that the forest industry firms have made a careful calculation of the most profitable level of forest inventory, then perhaps this could serve as a rough standard for other classes of ownership. At present stumpage prices, even allowing for the considerable time required to reduce national forest inventory by 40 percent, the present value of those 400 billion board feet of "excess inventory" is at least $12 billion, and based on 5 percent interest—a rate well below current levels—the annual cost of this "excess inventory" is $600 million.

This type of calculation could be approached in other ways. For instance, the inventory on national forests might be reduced until the present annual growth was 2.5 percent of standing timber (the average relationship for all forests) instead of the 1.0 percent actually found in 1970; this would mean a reduction of 60 percent in inven-

[2] The data in tables 7 and 8 on pages 59 and 61 can be used for this calculation.

tory on national forests. If annual timber growth on national forests were doubled as a result of harvesting some mature stands and replacing them with faster growing younger stands and by practicing more intensive forestry, and if inventory were held at the level of the average relationship to annual growth, this would mean a reduction in inventory by more than a fourth, perhaps as much as a third, of its present volume.

Still another approach to estimation of optimum timber inventory on national forests is to calculate growth-age relationships for each forest type and site class, and to harvest timber at the age when the annual growth in value just equalled the annual cost, including the interest return on the value of the timber that could be harvested—this is financial maturity. From these data, optimum inventory could be calculated for each forest of mixed ages. This would almost surely reveal even more "excess inventory" than the simple calculations above.

The specifics of this type of calculation can doubtless be greatly improved. In addition to being applied by forest type, site class, and region, they could also be made with stumpage at different prices and with different interest rates. However such calculations may be made, they will show that the cost of carrying the present volumes of old growth timber on national forests is very high—several hundreds of millions of dollars annually. This is an inevitable result of the Forest Service policy of slow harvest of the mature old growth timber. Some persons may assert that there is great value, not monetary but in some human terms, to the preservation of old growth forests. If this be granted, how much volume should be so maintained in order to produce these values? And who pays the costs?

One reason that annual net growth and annual harvest on national forests is so low is that so many of the old trees die every year, but the logs are not harvested due in part to lack of accessibility. In the fall of 1973, the General Accounting Office (GAO) chided the Forest Service for the low harvest of this salvage timber. According to Forest Service data, about 6 billion feet of sawtimber on national forests die each year; this is equal to nearly 50 percent of the allowable cut from national forests as presently calculated. All of this salvage timber could not be harvested, no matter how much effort was made to do so, but the GAO argued that far more could be harvested than in fact was harvested. In well-managed forests where all trees were of growing ages and sizes, the amount of such dead salvageable timber would be negligible.

This excess inventory of growing stock on national forests is particularly ironic in view of the serious lack of investment and management funds for these forests. Almost all groups concerned to have national forests managed more for their particular interest will agree that the total funds available to the Forest Service have been inadequate.

The matter of national forest management costs possibly being excessive is much harder for an outsider to judge. The Forest Service has a reputation, widely believed to be merited, of being as efficient as any government agency. Its personnel are universally conceded to be honest and dedicated. It surely strives for efficiency, as the reading of its various reports will show. One thus hesitates to suggest that costs of national forest management are far too high in relation to results achieved, but several other facts must be looked at also:

1. Except for a few years in the 1950s, the cash costs of managing the national forests (including constructing needed roads) have exceeded cash receipts from all sources. The latter include low or no amounts for many of the goods and services produced on national forests which are not sold for cash or for which the prices are far below a competitive market level. But "shadow prices" for these outputs would have to be put at what seem, intuitively, impossibly high figures to make receipts equal operating costs. Moreover, this type of comparison makes no allowance for the use of the immense wealth bound up in the national forests—billions of dollars worth of timber, land, and other resources. A reasonable interest charge on the present worth of the national forests is much greater than the annual cash receipts from national forests. A manager who cannot make a highly valuable estate even pay its way in terms of cash operating costs, surely must expect some criticism on this basis.

2. Some other publicly owned forests do vastly better, as far as cash management costs in relation to cash revenue are concerned. The State of Washington, for example, operates its forest lands to provide a substantial net revenue to the school system of the state. The Bureau of Land Management operates forest lands at a much lower ratio of cash costs to cash income than do the national forests. Some other public forests in the United States provide net cash revenues over management costs.

3. It is gravely to be doubted that the large private forests of the country fail to produce a substantial net cash return from operations. While these private forest owners do not have all the management responsibilities encountered on the national forests, they do have to build roads, protect watersheds and wildlife at least to a degree, make their lands available for some public outdoor recreation, and otherwise encounter at least some of the national forest problems of management.

4. Disquieting stories are heard about national forest timber sales —apparently in large numbers and for considerable volumes of timber—where the cost of making the timber sale exceeded the receipts from the timber sold. To the extent that these stories are true, they reflect a highly inefficient situation—either the timber should not be sold at all, or some means should be found to reduce the costs drastically. Good forestry in a silvicultural sense may not be good forestry in an economic sense.

The Forest Service emerges from this analysis as a land-poor landlord, one who owns vast areas of valuable property but lacks cash to manage it well, and whose management produces low monetary returns. In chapter 10 we shall explore the extent to which these results on national forests are fairly chargeable to the Forest Service, and the degree to which they are fairly chargeable to other parts of the governmental apparatus.

National forest administration falls short of an economic optimum for several reasons:

1. Current investment in national forests for roads, for tree planting and other stand establishment, in forestry practices such as thinnings, in provision of outdoor recreation facilities, and in other activities is too low and often ill-directed among forests of different productive capacities.

2. There is no charge for interest and capital use on past investments or on the value of the presently standing timber; hence there is a strong built-in tendency to waste capital. Our foregoing calculations suggest that the annual cost of excessive capital may be greater than the annual value of timber sold from national forests.

3. The rate at which the mature old growth forests have been harvested has been too slow. This is another manifestation of the wasteful use of capital mentioned above, but this conservative harvesting program has also kept the growing of timber at far too low a level.

4. The lack of economic analysis of outputs from the national forests has led to decisions about these outputs which do not—and cannot—take economic values into account.

In thus stressing the problems of national forest management, one must not overlook the great achievements and contributions to good resource management which the Forest Service has made in the past. But most of those contributions to resource utilization were developed during decades when the Forest Service was not really faced with the problems of economic management of the output of national forests, and when the role of the national forests in the wood supply of the nation was much smaller than today. With changing times come new responsibilities. The national forests today do not, in general, have timber management superior to that on the forest industry forests, and the quality of the silviculture on the national forests as a whole lags behind that on the best industrial forests. To a large extent, this is not the fault of the Forest Service; the tools it has been given to work with are inadequate for the present and for the future.

A NATIONAL SCALE FOR
MULTIPLE USE OF FORESTS

Multiple use of forest lands often means the integration of various uses on closely intermingled lands or on the same land at different times. The scale at which multiple forest use should be planned and implemented is an important matter with significant economic overtones. The concept of multiple use often finds application through a local forest management unit—the ownership unit for a small private forest owner, a ranger district in a national forest, or other similar unit. This type of multiple forest use planning and management is important, but multiple forest land use planning and management is also important at a national scale. One can use the information presented in this and preceding chapters to sketch out a national system of multiple forest land use whereby some land would be used for some purposes and other land for other purposes.

Suppose, for instance, that an effort were made to produce a substantial volume of wood annually—as much as there seemed an economic market for—on a relatively small acreage of forest land by means of intensive forestry, and that the rest of the land were devoted to forest uses other than wood production. What kind of a model or "scenario" might one devise? One such scenario might be based on forest ownership class and wood productivity classification, and one might put some of the forest land into intensive forestry, some into careful "natural" forestry, some into a deferred harvest classification, and some into more or less permanent reservation. It is possible to develop a "low-acreage high-intensity" model which would produce more wood annually than was actually grown in 1970 and use only about 40 percent of the commercial forest acreage of the United States (table 14). This model contemplates setting aside all the productivity site class V lands for uses other than wood production and putting substantial proportions of other site classes into a withdrawn or a deferred classification, while at the same time practicing intensive forestry on the more productive sites. According to calculations summarized earlier, this wood production would be economically feasible. The land on

Table 14. A Forest Management Model for Low-Acreage, High-Intensity Wood Production in the United States

| Site class | Ownership | Forest area in each management class (.........percent of total.........) | | | | Annual wood growth (.....bill. cu. ft.....) | | Forest acreage | |
|---|---|---|---|---|---|---|---|---|---|
| | | Intensive | Natural | Deferred | Withdrawn | Harvested | Deferred or withdrawn | Subject to regular harvest (.....mill. acres.....) | Deferred or withdrawn |
| I to III | Forest industry | 80 | 20 | 0 | 0 | 6.0 | 0 | 31.0 | 0 |
| | All public | 50 | 40 | 10 | 0 | 5.8 | 0.3 | 36.5 | 4.0 |
| | Other private | 20 | 40 | 40 | 0 | 7.4 | 3.2 | 57.7 | 38.5 |
| IV | Forest industry | 50 | 40 | 10 | 0 | 2.0 | 0.1 | 22.4 | 2.5 |
| | All public | 0 | 40 | 40 | 20 | 0.9 | 1.4 | 19.8 | 29.6 |
| | Other private | 0 | 10 | 50 | 40 | 0.6 | 5.2 | 12.1 | 109.1 |
| V | Forest industry | 0 | 0 | 40 | 60 | 0 | 0.3 | 0 | 11.4 |
| | All public | 0 | 0 | 0 | 100 | 0 | 1.0 | 0 | 41.2 |
| | Other private | 0 | 0 | 0 | 100 | 0 | 1.9 | 0 | 78.8 |
| All | All | | | | | 22.7 | 13.4 | 179.5 | 315.1 |

Note: The model is based on a program designed to maximize wood output from the best forest sites and deferment or reservation of harvest on less productive sites.

which timber was grown for harvest would have important non-wood outputs, such as wildlife and watershed values, but most importantly, a very large proportion of the total commercial forest acreage would be available for nonharvest uses and outputs.

This particular model might not be effectuated—numerous variations are possible—but the essential point is that the great wood-production possibilities of intensive forestry on the better forest sites open up enormous opportunities for multiple use forestry on a national scale. That is, some land can be used for one purpose, other land can be used for other purposes, each with various subsidiary uses; the whole would be very much a multiple use forestry management, even though every forested acre does not have every forest use every year.

Table 14 is concerned only with the growing of wood, on a long term basis. It does not face the problems of harvesting wood from existing stands or from sites of different productive capability. It does not provide an economic incentive to private forest landowners to forego timber harvest on their lands of low productivity. It presents a national picture only; somewhat different multiple use programs might be necessary regionally, due in large part to the dependence of local economies on timber from less productive sites. This "scenario" is thus suggestive rather than definitive. But, with such very great potential for increased timber output from smaller areas by means of intensive forestry, the possibilities of reconciling competing demands for forest land are significantly greater than would be the case if timber output were constrained to present levels.

## SPECIAL PROBLEMS OF FOREIGN TRADE
IN FOREST PRODUCTS

Several policy issues have arisen regarding foreign trade in forest products, which involve questions of economic efficiency. Except for softwood plywood (on which there is an effective duty), trade in wood products between the United States and other countries faces few tariff or other barriers. But most wood products are relatively heavy for their value and cannot be economically transported far by land; by water, transport costs relate largely to loading and unloading and much less to distance, hence wood products can often move relatively long distances by water. The United States is a net importer of wood and products made from wood fiber; in 1971, total imports equalled 2,800 million cubic feet of roundwood (or its equivalent in manufactured products), and exports totalled about 1,500 million cubic feet, leaving a net import balance of almost 1,300 million cubic feet. But this situation differed greatly according to product, to origin, and to destination. About seven major import or export situations for wood and its products can be recognized:

1. The United States imports most of the hardwood plywood it consumes—mostly from the Pacific Basin—and also some hardwood veneer and lumber; annual imports of this kind run to less than 300 million cubic feet (roundwood equivalent). There has been no significant controversy over these imports, partly because the specific products involved are not produced in the United States, and partly because there seems to have been little concern for the environmental aspects of such imports.

2. The United States imports paper and some pulpwood, chiefly from eastern Canada. This is a good source of relatively good paper, closer to many American consuming centers than any American source, and relatively cheaper than comparable American papers would be. There has been no significant controversy regarding these imports. Their volume has been about 1,200 million cubic feet (roundwood equivalent) annually.

3. The United States imports lumber from Douglas fir and other softwood species from western Canada; the lumber is similar to that produced in the Pacific Northwest. The Canadian producers have some advantages, including their ability to ship lumber by water from the coastal region to the East Coast of the United States at the cheapest rates available; American producers are limited by the Jones Act to shipping in American-owned and American-manned vessels, and the freight rates are usually prohibitive. Interior British Columbian lumber, predominantly white spruce, moves by rail to U.S. markets. There has been little controversy about this lumber—we have been anxious to get it for the most part. Such imports in recent years have been about 1,200 million cubic feet (roundwood equivalent), or about the same as the paper and paper-related imports from eastern Canada.

4. The United States exports paper, paperboard, and a little pulp and pulpwood (the latter chiefly to Canada). Much of this goes to western Europe, where we seem to have a competitive strength compared with other sources of supply. The volume in recent years of all these exports has been about 550 million cubic feet (roundwood equivalent), and there has been no significant controversy regarding these exports. The main wood involved is one of the Southern pines, mostly grown in the southeastern United States, and the exports help to make intensive forestry of this type profitable there.

5. In recent years the United States has developed significant ex-

ports in wood chips to Japan; they come from the Pacific Northwest. For the most part, the chips represent wood which has no other economic use—mill wastes, small materials from the woods, less desired species, and so forth. While this type of material is used by pulp mills in the Northwest, the capacity and output of such mills is not great enough to absorb all the chips that can be produced, largely because such mills cannot compete effectively in the eastern U.S. markets because of freight costs. Development of a market for these chips has undoubtedly stimulated more intensive use of the wood grown in the forests, and the volume of such exports in recent years has been about 100 million cubic feet (roundwood equivalent). While there has been some criticism of this type of export, its advantages have been so widely hailed that it has not been a major controversial issue.

6. Lumber and pulp or paper have been exported from Alaska, almost wholly to Japan. Because of freight costs, these wood products cannot economically be brought to the conterminous United States, again because of the Jones Act. Export of logs from federal lands (nearly the whole of the supply) is prohibited in Alaska; logs from federal lands must receive primary manufacture in Alaska. While there has been some criticism of exports, the fact that the wood would be unavailable to the rest of the United States in any case has muted the controversy about export—there has been other controversy about methods of harvesting this timber, or indeed, whether to harvest it at all. The volume of such exports has been about 160 million cubic feet (roundwood equivalent).

7. This brings us to the last and most bitterly controversial of the U.S. foreign trade movements of wood—the export of whole logs or of square-sawed cants from the Pacific Northwest to Japan. These exports have increased rapidly in recent years to about 400 million cubic feet (roundwood equivalent) in 1971 and more in 1972. The Japanese prefer to buy logs or cants rather than manufactured products, such as lumber, because they saw such logs to their own specifications and dimensions. Some of the logs so exported have been hemlock, a species not in the highest demand in the United States, and some have been Douglas fir; all have come from the Pacific Northwest and northern California. When lumber and plywood prices have been high and/or supplies short, those having difficulty getting supplies at what they consider reasonable prices have proposed a limitation or even an embargo against log exports to Japan. They have been joined by mill owners dependent upon purchased logs, who wanted to protect their supply sources. These groups did succeed in getting a legislative limitation in volume of

logs from federal lands that could be exported, and the logs actually exported came from private and state land. Environmentalists opposed to the cutting of old growth forests have denounced the export of logs, arguing that harvests could be reduced if logs were not exported.

Several arguments have been advanced in favor of continued log exports to Japan. In the first place, if the Japanese could not buy logs, they would buy lumber, though this is less valuable to them because there is more wasted in resawing to their specifications; they would buy lumber in the United States if it were available (they have bought a little lumber here) and would buy more in British Columbia. Buying lumber instead of logs would mean more employment in the United States and a favorable effect on the balance of trade. British Columbia imposes no barrier to lumber exports; its barrier to log exports is limited to logs from Crown lands (nearly all of the total) and is to insure that these logs are manufactured in the Province. If the Japanese bought more Canadian lumber, there would be less lumber to export from Canada to the United States, and the United States would have gained no wood by an embargo on log exports. This is the classic argument against trying to limit exports when the country is a net importer—it gains nothing.

If log exports to Japan were limited or stopped, this would impose a burden on some U.S. forest owners, especially those producing species which the Japanese are eager to buy but which are in less active demand in the United States—hemlock, in particular. Loss of export markets would deprive producers of profitable outlets for logs during periods of slack U.S. demand for lumber. Finally, there is the general trade argument and the balance of payments problem. If the United States wishes to buy television sets, radios, autos, and other products from Japan, it must sell something to pay for these imports. The United States runs an adverse balance of trade with Japan, and if it were not for the U.S. exports of farm and forest commodities, that adverse balance of trade would be still more severe. The United States is one of the world's largest importers of raw materials; does it seek only to buy, and never to sell? What about our vaunted support of private business, private markets, and freer world trade?

Exports of logs to Japan raise another type of national policy consideration which has not, thus far at least, played a large part in the public debate over these exports. How far is the United States willing to expose its domestic consumers to world-wide competition for basic natural resource products? This issue is more important for agricultural than for forest products, but it is not unimportant for the latter. If the United States permits free export of agricultural commodities, as the market may dictate, the American housewife is in competition with Russian, Japanese, German, and other housewives for meat and other foods. In times of tight market supplies (as in 1972 and much of 1973), the effect upon prices to the American consumer can be severe. The effect of unlimited wood export to Japan or elsewhere might be severe in times of extremely high building activity in the United States—a situation which does not exist in 1974 because of the extremely high interest rates, but one which might recur in some later year. A protectionist sentiment is to be expected under these conditions. But the free trade argument applies here—if one is to buy abroad, one must also sell there. It is ironic that in this day and country of high industrial technology, the products of the soil have shown so much more competitive strength in international markets than have many products of the factory.

The arguments over log exports to Japan wax and wane, partly as lumber prices rise and fall. It is doubtful if such arguments will ever cease. However, the controversy over log exports must be seen in the context of larger national policy issues over international trade, and so far, those arguing for relatively free trade have won in actual market operations.

# 8.

## Who Gains and Who Pays?

Economic effficiency strives to secure the greatest output in relation to inputs; this is desirable, but it is not enough. Who benefits from resource utilization, and who bears its costs? This is a question of economic equity or economic welfare; in the formulation of policy, it is no less important than is economic efficiency.

Some inequality in gains, some inequality in bearing the costs, and some divergence between incidence of gains and of costs are perhaps inevitable for any public or private program. The complexities of our economic system, differences in natural ability and in inherited position and wealth of citizens, and simple chance all combine to produce inequalities in gains, costs, and gain-cost relations. There is not, and perhaps cannot be, any such neat test for economic equity as there is for economic efficiency. For the latter, gains and costs can be evaluated (sometimes with difficulty and dubious accuracy) and a balance struck, but gains and losses in economic welfare are more elusive, and "balance" is more difficult to define. Gross inequalities in gains, or in sharing of costs, or of relationship between gains and costs, will offend many individuals and societies. But what is "gross," in this context? What is the optimum degree of inequality?

There is simply no neat answer. The analyst can strive to describe the inequalities which do exist, or those which would exist if some particular resource program were followed, in order to sharpen the issues and define the choices society must make as to the degree of inequality it seeks or will tolerate. Even such a descriptive process may well tax our analytical powers to the utmost.

GAINERS FROM FOREST OUTPUTS

The gainers from forest production may be classified or grouped in various ways. First of all, as to their position in the overall economic structure: some forest users are consumers, as is the family using the forest for recreation purposes; some are producers of materials or services for other consumer groups, as is the timber processor, who does not consume the lumber he makes but instead sells it (through various intermediaries) to a final consumer of paper or lumber; and some are suppliers of goods and services to forest users, as is the outfitter who relies upon wilderness users for his business. The latter may be as dependent upon the forest as any direct user, but his use is once removed from the forest.

Gainers from forest production may also be classified according to their geographical location into local, regional, and national gainers. There is considerable correlation between directness of gain and closeness of location, that is, the local resident is in a better position to use the local forest for recreation than is the distant city dweller; the local wood processing plant and its employees are more directly dependent upon the local forest than is the distant wood user who may have alternative sources of supply, and so on. For forest production, as for many other kinds of natural resource use, there is no necessary correspondence between local gains and national gains; a program may greatly benefit a local area but have limited—or even negative—values nationally, or some program may be nationally efficient but create severe local problems.

Gainers from forest production may also be classified temporally into those who gain today, those who gain tomorrow, and those who gain in the next generation. This is a problem common to many resource situations in addition to forests. How far shall the demands and needs of future generations be a determinant of or an influence on current decisions?

Who gains from forest output depends in part, but only in part, upon who owns the forest. The private forest owner gains many of the outputs of his forest but he cannot, or in practice does not, capture all of them. It is precisely this externality of benefit which creates some of the forest management problems for private forest owners. Forests owned by the public—by government at some level —are used by private individuals, and the use is rarely, if ever, exactly in proportion to the way costs of government are born. Thus, both private and public forests have divergences between gains and costs of forest ownership.

The individual or the family which enjoys outdoor recreation in a forest setting, whether a publicly or a privately owned forest, is a direct user, hence a direct gainer, of this forest output. The business which supplies such users with recreation equipment, supplies, food, fuel, and other items, including sometimes direct personal service as guides, is also a gainer, though not a direct consumer of forest output. We know very little about these consumers. There are data on numbers of "visits" to national forests, national parks, state forests, state parks, and other publicly owned areas, but such data have serious weaknesses. Many such public areas are not truly forests; for instance, only half of the total national forest area is commercial forest (and much is site class V, which I think is not truly commercial forest). We do not know what proportion of the recreation visits are to forested areas and what proportion are to nonforested areas, and we do not know how many individuals visit forests. "Visits" count each person each time he or she comes to the area. There is a substantial but unknown duplication, since many people visit such areas more than once during the year or visit more than one kind of area. Perhaps half of the individuals in the United States visit some publicly owned forest each year. There is even less information about the use of private forests for outdoor recreation; a few large forest owners estimate such statistics, but there are almost no data on visits to the large number of small private forests for which outdoor recreation is presumably one major purpose of ownership.

The use of forests for outdoor recreation is markedly affected by the distance the user lives from the forest; use, in terms of total visits per 1,000 population, declines rapidly as distance increases. This is the distance-decay function which applies to many economic activities. It applies to forests owned primarily for recreation as well as to forests owned primarily for other purposes; if one buys a piece of forested property for his personal recreation, he prefers it where he can get to it for weekends and other frequent use. Nationally famous areas, such as some of the national parks and some of the national forests, will draw some visitors from a distance; the redwoods, for instance, draw visitors from a long distance. But even for these forests, the distance-decay function still operates—its slope and co-ordinates are different from those for a less outstanding forest, but people who live within a few hundred miles will come more frequently than people who live a few thousand miles away.

Wilderness users are similar in many ways to general recreation users, but of course on a vastly smaller scale of activity. In 1970 there were 6 million visits recorded to the designated wilderness areas of the national forests; data are not available for use of the so-called "de facto" wilderness areas of the national forests or for designated wilderness areas of other federal lands. As with general recreation use, these data on numbers of visits include each person each time he or she enters a wilderness area, and the numbers of individuals involved are less than visits by an unknown proportion. Some persons visit a wilderness area one year but not every year, hence the total number of persons who have ever visited a wilderness area, while unknown, is larger than the number visiting such areas in one year. But the total number of persons ever visiting wilderness areas must be a small fraction, perhaps no more than 3 to 5 percent, of the total population.

In addition to the direct users of wilderness areas, some people—perhaps a good many—take satisfaction in the existence of a wilderness area even though they have never visited it, and even though they do not expect ever to visit it in the future. They find it reassuring simply to "know that it is there." Protagonists for wilderness make a good deal of this type of demand. Surely it exists, as it may well exist for many other kinds of natural or man made resource situations, but measurement of its strength is difficult and perhaps impossible. Many people will assert such an interest until some suggestion is made that they pay for this type of satisfaction.

Various sample studies have been made of wilderness users. In general, they are persons in the active years of life—comparatively few are very young or very old persons—above average in education; somewhat above average in income, but not rich; and often reside at considerable distances from the wilderness area because the distribution of wilderness and of population in the United States is so very different. But the distance-decay function applies to wilderness use of forests as it does to general recreation use.

The many kinds of wildlife and the varying conditions under which they live and thrive make generalizations about them difficult. The value of the wildlife arises out of the way persons regard it. The uses of wildlife in the forest fall generally into consumptive and nonconsumptive categories. Hunting and fishing are the two chief activities of consumptive use. Even when hunting results in the death of the wildlife species concerned, it is not clear that it reduces the number of animals living in the forest. That is, in the absence of hunting, starvation might well keep deer or other wildlife species to the same limits. The nonconsumptive uses of wildlife include simple viewing and photographing; they extend to many species which are not hunted.

There are few data on enjoyment of wildlife in forests. There are some data on numbers of hunters and fishermen and on numbers of hunting and fishing licenses sold, but these generally do not distinguish between forested and nonforested situations—the same hunter may hunt in open fields and forests alike. Most of the enjoyment of wildlife in forest settings is reflected in the figures (with all their deficiencies) on numbers of recreation and wilderness visits.

It is even more difficult to define who gains from the existence or the preservation of a general forest environment. Those persons who actually enter the forests on foot are likely to be counted as recreation visits, described above; other persons will drive through forested areas, not leaving their cars at all or merely stopping briefly at lookout points, and these normally are not included as recreation visits; still others will take significant satisfaction from the existence of forests even though they rarely visit or see them.

The difficulty of identifying gainers from the recreation output of forests applies also to the conservation of the forest or the prevention of soil erosion within forests. It is hard to isolate direct "users" of such output of the forest; in a sense, everyone is a "gainer" when the forest is maintained in a healthy condition. But again, while not easy to measure, such values cannot be ignored.

Water users are a diverse group—irrigation farmers, electric utilities, industry, and households. Actually everyone is a water user. Most water flowing from forested areas, whether on privately or publicly owned land, is incidental to other forest outputs and values. That is, little direct effort has been made to secure this water supply, though some efforts may have been made to protect its quality. Much of the total water supply of the nation, but far from all of it, comes from forested areas. In a very general sense, the watershed function of forests touches most of the national population, but most people are quite unaware of this relationship with forests. They are outraged, of course, if their water supply is cut off, or if the water quality deteriorates noticeably, but they are unlikely to view this as forestry-connected.

The direct and indirect gainers from wood production in forests are numerous and diverse groups of people. In 1967 there were over 10,000 sawmills in the United States. Many of these were small—over half had four or fewer employees, and 92 percent had fewer than fifty employees—and these small mills produced but 5 percent and 36 percent, respectively, of the value of the wood products from sawmills. In many parts of the country, especially the South and the Northeast, small portable sawmills are established by a worker and a few associates to saw a relatively small volume of timber from some privately owned forest. While many such mills do a poor job, technically speaking, they do produce a good deal of lumber, often from timber stands that would not interest larger mills, and they provide much needed local employment. A comparatively few large mills produce most of the lumber and plywood. In contrast to the sawmill situation, there are but 411 pulp mills in the United States. While these also vary in size, the minimum size of a mill which makes pulp is vastly larger than the minimum size of a mill which can manufacture lumber.

For both sawmills and papermills, there is a substantial employment of men in the woods, harvesting the trees and hauling them to the mills. There are also other men engaged in timber buying and selling. To these must, of course, be added the considerable employment within the mills themselves. In addition to all these persons directly employed in wood harvest and manufacture, a substantial number of men and women are engaged in providing services both to the wood harvesting and manufacturing processes, and to the men employed directly therein. Once the lumber or the paper leaves the mill, additional employment is provided in its transport, storage, marketing, and other necessary activities. All of this employment is directly connected with wood as a raw material. There is still more employment created indirectly, such as in printing and other paper use and in construction and other lumber and plywood uses. All in all, as wood products progress from tree to final consumer, they involve the employment of rather large numbers of persons.

Wood, as lumber or as plywood, is directly involved in new construction, even when most of the construction material is steel, concrete, and stone. The number of new dwelling units constructed annually rarely exceeds 3 percent of the standing stock of dwelling units, but this does not mean that the number of persons directly interested in new construction is only 3 percent of the total population. Most new dwelling construction is for persons of average or higher incomes, whether they buy or rent; some, it is true, may be publicly subsidized for lower income groups, but this has been and is likely to continue to be by far the smaller proportion of the total. The persons buying or renting these new dwelling units vacate other living space, and this in turn is taken by persons who vacate still other space, until ultimately there may be a dozen families involved for each new dwelling unit. It is the lower income but unsubsidized families who have the greatest stake in an adequate level of new housing construction; if the trickle-down process is to work to help those at the end of the line, there must be a substantial input at the beginning of the line. The beneficiaries of an adequate supply of lumber and plywood building materials from the forest are thus far removed from the forest physically, unlikely to use it for recreation or other purposes (most unlikely to use it as wilderness), and unlikely to fully realize their dependence upon wood production and harvest.

WHO PAYS FOR FOREST OUTPUTS?

The values gained from forests, regardless of the form of those gains and regardless of the identity of the persons securing them, can be paid for in one or a combination of several ways. One of the simplest ways is direct payment, at the time and place of getting the forest output, of an amount determined in relation to the quantity of the output or the value of the gain from forest use. The buyer of wood who pays per cord or per 1,000 board feet, the recreationist who pays an entrance fee or user charge, and many others fall into this grouping. The amount of the payment may be determined by a more or less competitive market or by administrative action; it may represent the full value of the service or something less; and it may cover the costs (however these are measured) of providing the service or it may not. The distinguishing characteristic of this method is not the amount of the payment, absolutely or in relation to some value or cost, but the fact that the payment is made at the time and point of use and in proportion to volume of use.

Values of forest output may be paid for by paying the costs of forest ownership—taxes, forest protection costs, interest on capital, and the like. This what the small private forest owner, who regards his forest primarily as a place for personal recreation, does. But it is also what society does in paying for publicly owned forests used for many purposes, especially when the full costs of such ownership are not recovered from the direct forest users. The forest industry firm which grows sawlogs or pulpwood on its own forests for its own processing is also paying for this wood by these costs of forest ownership; use of wood by the mill may or may not involve an accounting charge crediting the value of the wood to the woods operation, but normally there is no actual cash payment from one party to another.

Society, through taxation, pays some forestry costs both on publicly owned lands and in aids to owners of private forests; the latter may be direct aids such as provision of planting stock or provision of technical services. There are numerous difficult problems of taxation involving forests. Do privately owned forests pay taxes for general governmental operations that are proportionate to their reasonable obligations?

Society can pay in other and more subtle ways for wood, or for its lack. If there is an ample supply of all wood products at reasonable prices, then many segments of society gain—in all the many uses of wood suggested above. In contrast, if wood supply is severely limited and/or high in price, then society as a whole is poorer—regardless of the forest production financial account for either private or public forests. If wood supply is inadequate, production of dwelling units and other structures is inhibited, or substitute materials (nearly all of which involve nonrenewable resources) must be used; in general society is worse off in a real sense. Though there may be neither cash paid out, nor taxes uncollected, society has paid by inadequate supplies of forest products and services.

For all of the outputs and uses of the forest except wood production—recreation, wilderness, wildlife, water, and so forth—payments at time of use and in proportion to use are small or nonexistent. Members of the public who use private forest land for recreation generally pay nothing for such use; payments for recreation use of publicly owned forest land are small, generally far below the value of such use. The same is true for wilderness use. There is no payment for the wildlife values created and none for the value of the water flowing from the land. The individual who uses his own forest for these purposes does pay its costs, though not at the time and place of use or in proportion to use; he incurs costs annually, and specific uses are generally without added costs.

A considerable part, but far from all, of the wood harvested from forests is paid for at the time and place of harvest and in proportion (more or less) to the volume of timber harvested. In 1970 some 18 billion board feet of softwood and hardwood sawtimber were harvested from forest industry forests. Although precise data on the accounting practices of these firms are unavailable, it may be assumed that most of this timber was not sold in an open market, but that accounting charges of some kind were made, from woods to mill, that may or may not have approximated market values of the timber involved. For the other 44 billion board feet of softwood and hardwood sawtimber harvested in that year from various public and other private forests, it may be assumed that some kind of direct cash payment was made, more or less at time and point of sale and more or less in proportion to volume harvested. On this basis, somewhat more than two-thirds of all timber harvested was paid for on this direct payment basis.

MATCHING OF GAINS AND COSTS

Some persons are in physical locations or otherwise personally so situated that they can gain far more from forest production of various kinds than can other persons. Hence a great disparity in gains from forest outputs necessarily exists among individuals in the total population. Likewise, some persons incur substantial costs for forest ownership, management, and use, while other persons incur very low costs—including some, as in taxes paid, that they do not recognize as forestry costs at all. Again, a great disparity among individuals necessarily exists in the bearing of forest costs. These disparities in gains and in costs apply both to publicly owned and to privately owned forests.

It is theoretically possible that the disparities in gains from forests would be exactly matched by the disparities in costs of forests, so that every individual had costs in exactly the same proportion to gains as did every other individual. But such precise matching certainly does not now exist, and the statistical odds of it ever occurring are very small indeed. A divergence between incidence of costs and distribution of gains exists now and is highly probable for the future.

If the costs of forest management and production were borne in exactly the same proportion as the benefits from such management, then equity questions would largely disappear. There would still be difficult questions of defining costs and gains, but at least theoretically the gains could be paid for fully. Thus, although one person would then enjoy either public or private forests far more than some other individual, it could be argued that he fully paid for this greater gain, and that the less advantageously placed person was at no net disadvantage. The latter might still argue that he was denied access to forest resources and thereby disadvantaged, but at least he would have to admit that the person getting the forest resources paid for them.

When the gains from forest use are not fully paid for—and, as we have seen, this is the case for many of the outputs of both private and public forests—then questions of both equity and efficiency arise. The person denied use of the forest outputs, for whatever reason, can fairly claim that the person who does get such outputs has gained an unfair and unreasonable economic advantage thereby. The person who gains some forest output at a price less than its value is tempted to use the resources for less valuable uses, and hence some inefficiency can creep in.

The users of forest outputs, both public and private forests, can be roughly and perhaps somewhat unfairly grouped into (1) "nonpaying guests" or "star boarders" or "freeloaders" and (2) payers. As we have noted, the only use of private and public forests which customarily pays most or all of its way is wood production. The other kinds of users will doubtless resent being called freeloaders, yet in fact they do not pay in any direct fashion for the gains they get from forest use. They may well argue that, as citizens, they bear a share of the costs of public forests, but it is hard to see how they can argue they bear a share of the costs of the private forests whose outputs they use at nominal charges or at none at all.

The people who gain use of public and private forests at nominal prices or without cost—the nonpaying guests—often incur other costs in connection with their activities in the forest. The wilderness user, for example, incurs cost for equipment and for travel. Likewise, the city or the irrigation district which does not pay for the water flowing from the forest may make large investments in dams and other structures in order to use that water. Substantial business enterprises may develop, in providing services to these various users of the forest. Of course, as I pointed out earlier in this chapter, wood production and harvest also provide substantial employment and business locally. The nonpaying guest is nonpaying only insofar as the forest resource is concerned; he usually must pay for the other associated services. In the economists' language, he pays no rent but he does pay for other inputs into his consumption process.

Outdoor recreation, wilderness area use, wildlife, general forest environment preservation, and conservation, whether on public or private land, are forest uses for which only a small part is paid directly—less, one judges, than 10 percent of either the cost of supplying the output or of its value. This is not to say that some individuals may not pay a lot more—someone may own a forest primarily to protect its wildlife, for his enjoyment or because he thinks some species should be protected for future generations. Most of those who want a forest environment preserved, including its aesthetic qualities which they value, pay nothing directly for this "use" of the forest.

Citizens pay for publicly owned forests through taxes in varying proportions depending on the tax system of the government concerned. Some small part of these taxes is used to maintain, operate, and manage the public forests, especially those producing forest outputs for which no direct payment is made by the user. To this extent, every citizen shares in the cost of providing these outputs of the public forests, but the citizen who does not secure any of these outputs—perhaps because he does not want them, perhaps because he lives where such outputs are practically unavailable—pays in exactly the same degree as the heavy consumer of such outputs, if their tax positions are the same.

Users of water flowing from forested areas by and large pay nothing for this water, as such. That is, they may incur considerable costs in diverting the water, or in conducting it to their homes or farms, or in storing it, but typically nothing for the water itself. The municipality that owns its own watershed for its municipal water supply is an exception, and many municipalities gain substantial water values from public forests.

The one use of the forest which does pay directly for the value of forest output is wood production; this is true for private and public forests alike. Wood producers (of various kinds) buy wood from private and public forests, or grow it on their own forests, and they pay, in one form or another for the wood obtained. This is not to assert that every buyer of national forest timber pays as much as he could or a "fair price"—however this might be defined—for every log he buys, or that full or "fair" prices are paid in all instances for private timber. Society as a whole, or taxpayers as a whole, bear some of the costs of timber growing on both public and private forests, but in general, wood users pay directly for the wood they use and pay for most if not all of its value.

# 9.

## Social or Cultural
## Acceptability of
## Forest Uses

Men do not seek to maximize their material well-being to the exclusion of all else. Everyone is Economic Man up to a point, but only
up to a point. Other considerations, such as personal philosophy or
ideology, religion, ethics, or other attitudinal relationships, or
social pressures of the group of which the individual is a member,
govern much individual conduct. Some of these cultural attitudes
are embodied in law, but many are not. Some things are simply done,
and others simply not done, as right and proper, either by the
standards of the individual or by the standards of the social community which become governing to the individual; these activities
are done or not done without regard to whether the doer is made
economically better off thereby. Most private charity, much religious
activity, and many other facets of life, modern or traditional, are
manifestations of the power of cultural or social attitudes.

Some economists would still say that the individual is motivated
by attempts to maximize his output, but that output is defined
to include these personal values as well as the material goods
and tangible services ordinarily capable of evaluation in a monetary
sense. One can indeed broaden the definition of economics to perfectly meaningless extremes—I suppose that all of courtship and of
sex could somehow be defined as an economic activity, if one tried
hard enough. But I prefer to consider cultural attitudes as a separate
factor or kind of factor. The problems and the necessities of considering kinds of forces and factors other than simple economic efficiency have been outlined, and need not be repeated.

Social or cultural acceptability is related to political acceptability.
As I use the terms, social acceptability is both wider and narrower
than political acceptability: wider, because social attitudes are often
made effective by means other than government or "politics"; narrower, because some of the political considerations relate to operational or administrative feasibility. The person who gives "politics"

as the reason why something cannot be done or why something else must be done, sometimes means that cultural attitudes of some part of the electorate are sufficiently strong and effective to force some line of action which pure economics would not have proposed. Sometimes, of course, "politics" means efforts by powerful figures to grab for themselves some of the benefits of particular courses of action; cultural acceptability for them is largely a matter of who gets the gravy.

Some major gradations or forms of cultural and social forces can be recognized:

1. A person or group advocates something, or denounces something else, or insists upon some kind of standards which will not meet tests of economic efficiency; this advocacy or denunciation or insistence is at a purely verbal level—perhaps full of sound and fury, not necessarily accomplishing anything.

2. Advocates may go one step further and not only offer or agree to pay the costs of the course they advocate—including loss of economic output because the advocated course is not the economic maximizing one—but actually establish a procedure or a process by which they will, in fact, bear such costs. One who does not share a particular set of cultural beliefs or standards is likely to be much more impressed by this stage than by the former.

3. The advocates seek to impose their standards and their will on others by law or by social pressures as effective as law. While persuasion may be necessary to secure the law or to make the social customs effective, the advocate seeks to go beyond persuasion and to compel compliance to his standards. In the early twentieth century, for instance, dedicated persons successfully sought to outlaw alcoholic beverages—to impose their standards of social conduct upon the whole nation. That effort ended in total failure, and at some considerable cost to the nation. The case for tight social controls is best when contrary actions, even by a minority, injure the majority or preclude some line of action sought by the majority.

SOME CULTURAL OR SOCIAL ISSUES IN FORESTRY

Various persons and groups have advocated certain forest uses and/or forestry practices on essentially cultural or social grounds. Only rarely have these uses or practices been chosen because they are economically efficient, although economics may be used as an argument when it seems to support a course advocated chiefly for other reasons. Some of these uses or practices have been advocated or are supported on grounds of physical and biological feasibility, but this line of support has also been secondary in most cases. These socially or culturally directed forest uses and practices have mostly been advocated for publicly owned forests, but to some extent for privately owned forests as well. In my scheme of values, cultural values or standards are as respectable a ground for advocacy of particular actions as is economic efficiency. However, not all specific proposals that are defended on cultural grounds are effective in realization of their purposes, and costs surely must be considered also.

Although several forest uses or practices might qualify for inclusion in this group, four situations have been the most important:

1. Wilderness preservation. There has been a powerful ideological or emotional content to the advocacy of wilderness withdrawals or "preservation." The Wilderness Act of 1964 was advocated as a means of giving legislative protection to areas which then had only administrative protection, and further extensions of the wilderness system were specifically precluded by the advocates. In more recent years, this position has been repudiated by advocates of major enlargements to the wilderness system. Some wilderness areas are defended on grounds that I call physical and biological feasibility— the importance of natural areas for research purposes, the importance of maintaining genetic strains found in the wilderness but not elsewhere, and the like. Wilderness area proposals are sometimes defended on economic grounds, such as the fact or the allegation that wilderness use is the highest and best use of a particular forested area, or on the ground that establishing a wilderness area preserves an option for the future, since the wilderness area could always be opened to exploitation, whereas a developed area could be returned to wilderness only with great difficulty. But to many wilderness advocates these arguments have been more crutches to support their advocacy than they have been guides to resource management. The question of who gains from wilderness and who pays for it has generally not been raised by the advocates but rather by the opponents of wilderness—the latter have argued that relatively few persons benefited while the costs were borne by someone else. It seems to me that the most accurate statement is that wilderness satisfies certain cultural standards or values of its advocates, and I do not see that any other ground for their advocacy is necessary. Others who do not share those values may oppose wilderness reservations on economic or other grounds.

2. Forest aesthetics or preservation of the general forest environment. To those whose personal ideologies place great stress on forest aesthetics, beauty and harmony exist in nature, but man is the de-

spoiler. Particular criticism has been directed at straight line borders to harvest cuts, as being aesthetically offensive. Likewise, slash, or tree tops and limbs left behind after timber harvest, has been denounced as aesthetically unacceptable. Still further, roads through forest areas have often been criticized as aesthetically offensive, as well as damaging to the soils, watersheds, and streams, especially when large scale cuts and fills were made or when the roads were highly visible on hillsides. Even one not highly sensitive or trained in such matters must concede that some of these criticisms are justified.

Various measures have been proposed, and used in some cases, to reduce the unaesthetic aftermath of timber harvest and other forest use. Such measures involve some costs or mean some income otherwise attainable is foregone. No measure of the economic values created by aesthetically directed practices has yet been devised, hence it is impossible to balance economic costs and returns from any practice or use which has an aesthetic objective. As with so many other situations, who gains from the forest use or practice, and who bears its costs? The aesthetic improvement secured by a modified timber harvest on a national forest may be gained primarily by local residents, who see the area often; the costs may fall on the national treasury and thus be borne by all citizens of the country, including many who have no idea what they are paying for. In other situations, the relationship between numbers of gainers and numbers of losers might be reversed, and many other situations are possible.

3. Clearcutting of timber, both as a special case of forest aesthetics and because of its own ill effects. The pros and cons of clearcutting were outlined in chapter 2 and need not be repeated here. Questions of who benefits and how much, and who pays and how much, from clearcutting have rarely been raised; or if raised, they have been overwhelmed by the graphics of the clearcut scene.

The arguments over clearcutting are often somewhat beside the point; the real issue is: Should the forest be cut at all? In some cases, present stands of trees might better be left uncut—where slopes are very steep, or where soils are thin, or where tree reproduction is uncertain, or where the standing trees have great values for some purpose such as stream protection. If the decision is made to cut, then the most appropriate method of cutting is indeed important; this depends upon the specifics of the site, the species, the stand, and the goal for the future forest.

It should also be recognized that any method of cutting may be carried out with skill and care, or badly and without concern for the site. Some of the horrible examples of clearcutting would be characterized by the advocates of clearcutting as unfortunate examples of a good practice badly misused. Selective cutting, which is one alternative way of removing mature trees in some situations, can also be carried out well or badly. When well done, it results in economic removal of some trees, preservation of others, a site which is less unattractive than a clearcut site, and a forest stand which will grow thriftily and produce the most valuable species and individual trees which the site is capable of. But selective cutting may be badly done; in fact, it often has been. A common type of selective cutting consists of taking out the best species and the best trees within each species. The forest as it previously existed is destroyed and its regeneration is more difficult than would be the case from clearcutting; some trees are preserved, but the original forest complex is sadly altered. This type of forestry practice has almost wholly escaped criticism on aesthetic, cultural, or social grounds, though it is widely criticized on silvicultural bases. Do those who find clearcutting so offensive not know what has happened in so much selective cutting, or are they satisfied with a cosmetic treatment of the forest? Even if the judgment about clearcutting on silvicultural and economic grounds is favorable, there is a high probability that the aesthetic or ideological attitude will not be.

4. Monoculture, or the growing of one species to the exclusion of all others. This practice is widely condemned by ecologists, whether it is on farms or in forests. The richness of plant associations, with their complementary as well as competitive relationships, and the richness of insect, bird, and animal life is much diminished in a monoculture. The farmer seeks a monoculture; he grows a crop for harvest and tries to exclude weeds and other plants and also various forms of insect and animal life harmful to his crop. Forests differ greatly in the richness of their plant cover. Dense natural lodgepole pine stands have very little other vegetation within the forest and consequently a modest variety of other life; the mixed natural hardwood stands of many parts of the eastern United States grow along with a dozen or more tree species and several kinds of shrubs, grasses, or forbs on the forest floor, and they attract a wide variety of bird, animal, and insect life. But forest monocultures, or something very close to them, may exist for small areas in nature where a particular species wholly dominates.

Growing trees in a monoculture is rarely easy, especially for more than very small areas—too many other species, including unwanted ones, intrude. When former farm fields, clean-cultivated for years, are planted to one of the southern pines, the initial result may be a monoculture or very close to it. But when a forested area is harvested and then planted, various species of trees and shrubs will almost surely be found—they seed in naturally from surrounding areas or sprout from stumps. It is true that, in many situations, forests can be established after the former forest was harvested or as the land is converted from farm crop production to forestry, and these will have far less plant diversity than will "natural" forests in the same area; as a result, bird, animal, and insect diversity will also be less. To many ecologists, this is undesirable. They might have tolerated a naturally seeding forest which had a limited species composition, but be dissatisfied with a man-planted forest of the same species composition.

Other instances of social or cultural objection or judgment about forestry situations or practices could be cited, but the foregoing will illustrate the kinds of situations which arise, as well as include the majority of such situations. Some generalizations might be drawn about these situations:

1. All involve "freeloading" in the sense this term was developed in chapter 8; in each case, some person or group advocates or demands some forestry practice (or the cessation of some other practice) but does not directly pay the costs involved, whether those costs are monetary or otherwise. He bears some costs as a taxpayer, but no more than another person who paid the same taxes and did not seek these forestry practices.

2. To put the same point in another way, all of the instances described here still belong in the first type of social attitude described above. Each is still in the talk stage; none has moved to the stage where the advocates are paying the bill directly, and none has moved (yet) to the stage of prohibitive legislation. There has been some talk both of payment and of legislation, but so far it is only talk. One cannot, of course, be sure what the future will bring in these respects.

3. Most of the attention of these proponents of social or cultural attitude has been directed toward the publicly owned forests. These have sometimes been described by the proponents of these attitudes as "our forests," which in part they are; but it is often overlooked that they are equally the forests of those who disagree with these social or cultural attitudes. There has been criticism of private forestry too. While the rights of private forest owners to carry out legal forestry on their own lands is recognized, the criticism of clearcutting, monoculture, and other forestry practices has extended to private forests also. And, of course, social attitudes might find expression in legislation which would control forest operations on private land.

The social and cultural attitudes toward forestry and forest practices, described so briefly in this chapter, are very powerful, must be considered in both public and private forestry in the future, and will almost certainly require major changes in the way forestry has been practiced in the past. The accuracy, relevance, and efficiency of such social attitudes are not really subject to tests of logic.

Do those who do not hold particular social or cultural attitudes toward forestry or forest practices have a right to demand that those who do bear the full costs—including income foregone—of their attitudes? Does any forest manager, public or private, have a right to operate without regard for the cultural attitudes of a significant fraction of the total citizenry?

It seems to me there is a great need for sociological research about cultural attitudes toward forests, forestry, and forest practices. We need to know, much more accurately than we now know, what public attitudes are, and to what extent they vary among groups according to the usual socioeconomic factors of age, education, income, social class, and the like. More importantly, we need to know why expressed attitudes are held, and what the trade-offs may be between cultural attitude and economic gains. Perhaps the day will come when forest sociology will be as well recognized as silviculture in the training and expertise of the forester. Until now, foresters and all the rest of us have relied too heavily upon "common knowledge" and intuition; cultural attitudes toward forestry are as capable of enlightening research as are any biological aspect of the forest.

# 10.

Operational
or Administrative
Practicality of
Forest Policy

Operational or administrative practicality is the last of the five standards or tests of forest policy which were outlined in chapter 3. Having considered the physical and biological feasibility and consequences of various forest management alternatives, having measured their economic efficiency, having estimated the distribution of gains and costs from each, and having considered the cultural or social acceptability of each, the hard question remains: Can we (as a nation, group, or organization) actually do what we decide we want to do? Have we the skill and the competence, given the framework within which we must operate, to carry out the policies we decide upon? Are we prepared to exert the necessary effort to implement policies? If not, then the policy decision is worthless. Indeed, it may well be argued that a policy decision which cannot or will not be carried out is worse than worthless, for it misleads some persons—perhaps many persons—into thinking that something is going to happen which, in fact, cannot happen. An inoperative forest policy is analogous to an inoperative fire department—it lulls the householder into a false security with a rude awakening when a fire occurs.

## SOME GENERAL CONSIDERATIONS

If a forest policy (of any specific kind) is to be carried out, then certain requirements must be met:

1. There must be a competent decision-making apparatus. Some way must exist to have policy issues recognized as such, to have them brought up for serious consideration at policy making levels (in the society, agency, company, or whatever), to have reasonably attainable facts gathered which will help arrive at a considered decision, to have the policy issues debated adequately, and to have a decision reached which is the best that one could expect under the

circumstances. The decision making must thus be considered, explicit, and intentional, rather than offhand, by default, or incidental to other operations. A good decision-making apparatus does not, of course, guarantee wise decisions; nor are the latter wholly precluded by a poor decision-making apparatus. But experience has shown that the probability of good decisions is greatly increased if the apparatus is good, compared with the results when the apparatus is faulty in one or more respects.

2. Equally, there must exist a good decision-implementing apparatus. The organization must be equal to the tasks which are put to it, that is, there must be adequate ways of translating general decisions into specific actions. There often is more than one way of doing a job, whatever it is, but the organization must be adequate. This is, of course, a major part of administration, whether public or private.

3. But there must also be some mechanism for continuing supervision, for inspection of operations and of results, and for review of procedures and even of objectives. Even the best organizations do not work perfectly at all times. Every good manufacturing process has tests for quality control, and administrative organizations equally need tests to control the results of their work. There must be a feedback from operations to policy making and policy implementing; what seemed like good policies may develop undesired side effects, or new possibilities may open up as a result of experience, or for other reasons the original policy must be changed as a result of experience. Feedback and supervision should not be left to chance, but the organization should be built to achieve them regularly and almost automatically.

4. Lastly, if policies are actually to be carried out, then men, materials, and money must be provided in adequate amounts and at the time they are needed.

There are a number of reasons, somewhat independent but also somewhat overlapping, why a forest policy, once decided upon, cannot or will not be carried out:

1. There may be a serious lack of any of the foregoing necessary elements to a successful implementation of a forest policy.

2. In particular, there may be a division of authority within and between the decision-making and decision-implementing processes, with no way to force a resolution of the differences among policy makers and no way to implement a decision. This is particularly likely to occur with public agencies; the checks and balances built into government to reduce the possibilities of dictatorial or single-person action all too often mean that firm decisions are not reached, or that what seem like decisions are not or cannot be carried out.

3. There may be resistance to a policy, even when it is arrived at by the best possible mechanisms. This resistance may range from grudging assent to the policy, with resultant lack of efficiency in operation, to outright sabotage. Sometimes there will be individuals in an organization (whether public or private) who do not agree with some policy and lack the power to stop its formal adoption but are prepared to try to stop the implementation of the policy, even to the extent of sabotage. Their sincerity and idealism may be high or they may be operating from rather narrow, selfish motives. Every administrator knows that there may be a world of difference between a policy as adopted at the top of an organization and the policy actually carried out by the men and women at the operating level; every well-run organization goes to some pains to try to enlist genuine cooperation from the rank and file of its employees.

4. The processes of decision making and decision implementing may be too cumbersome for the policies to be carried out well. In particular, the processes may work too slowly and yield too little. This deficiency is particularly likely to exist with public agency actions. The decision might be adequate in content, but if the timing is bad, the overall result is bad—for instance, forest nurseries must have money to produce seedlings ready to plant when a tract is logged, not three years afterward.

5. Closely similar to the above, there may be a deeply entrenched bureaucracy, whose methods of operation and whose attitudes toward the job were formed long ago, and which now resists changes that a new policy requires. While this is more common in public agencies, where employees are protected by tenure arrangements, this problem is not unknown in private organizations as well. Sometimes it arises out of professional training, professional experience, and professional standards. The forester who sets out a logging operation for maximum efficiency of harvesting costs without regard to aesthetic results, the logging engineer who lays out the road for maximum hauling efficiency without regard to soil erosion hazards, and many other employees carrying out specific tasks may be only translating the principles they learned long ago into specific present actions. Their motivations may be high, but they are out of step with the decision-making process of their organization.

6. Lastly, there may be a lack of specific tools, including money and men, for carrying out the policy. Forestry is particularly tempting to narrowly geared budget makers. Expenditures for tree planting, forest improvement, or other forest practices often do not seem to pay off for many years, hence seem postponable or of lower urgency. This attitude overlooks the fact that willingness and ability

to harvest presently standing trees may depend, quite properly, on steps taken now to grow trees for future harvest.

The matter of operational or administrative practicality applies to private as well as to public forests. I well remember the representative of a large forest industry company stating that he had given up trying to collect fees from recreationists using company forests, not because people were unwilling to pay and not because the sums were insignificant, but because his company had such a cumbersome bookkeeping procedure that both his field men and the recreationists rebelled at the paperwork in collecting a $2 daily recreation charge. Many a small private forest owner has reached some conclusion about what he would like to do with his forest only to be thwarted for lack of contracting firms or of workers to carry out the tasks. The Forest Service has repeatedly lacked appropriations adequate to do the jobs it felt were needed, at the scale and in the manner it wanted to do them. Examples of operational or administrative problems could be added for each major type of forest ownership.

If one emphasizes "practicality," then there is an obvious relationship with physical and biological feasibility on the one hand and with social or cultural acceptability on the other. It is impracticable to try to do what physically cannot be done or can be done only with the very greatest difficulty. Likewise, it may be impracticable to attempt some forest policy which is socially or culturally unacceptable. Social acceptability is not unchangeable, of course; given sufficient advantage in some line of action, attitudes toward it are likely to change. But, at any given moment, cultural attitudes are a fact of life and may be as difficult to change as the composition of the forest stand. The forest owner, whether private individual or public agency, may seek to change public attitudes; for example, he might try to show that in a given situation selective cutting may be preferable to clearcutting, while in another situation selective cutting may be more destructive to the true forest than clearcutting would be, and he may or may not succeed in changing social acceptability.

There is also a fairly clear relationship between operational or administrative practicality and politics, especially for publicly owned forests but for private ones too. The political process is one way in which social attitudes are made effective, though politics also has its own internal mechanisms, processes, motivations, and rewards. The operation of the political process may greatly affect the appropriations for a public forest agency, for instance, and sometimes largely irrespective of economic calculations; or the political process may lead to regulation of some aspects of private forest operations, such as effects upon stream flow, number of seed trees left per acre, or other factors.

## OPERATIONAL OR ADMINISTRATIVE PRACTICALITY, AS APPLIED TO FOREST INDUSTRY FORESTS

A forest industry firm has operational problems similar to those of private firms of the same size in other parts of the private economy. That is, it has decision making, decision implementing, supervision, and other problems, which are common to all private business firms. There seems little reason to think that these essentially business operations are more difficult for forestry than for other business. As far as an outsider can tell, a forest industry firm is able to carry out a realistic decision, once the decision is made.

To assert that the operational problems of forest industry firms are similar to, but no more difficult than, the operational problems of other private business does not, of course, say that forest industry firms do not face some special problems of other kinds. We have noted in earlier chapters that private industry forest firms have all the problems of physical and biological feasibility, economic efficiency, and cultural acceptability which face public agencies in forest management. In addition, the forest industry firms are unable to capture some of the values of their forest management, such as the watershed, wildlife, and recreational benefits, and sometimes they are unable to avoid some of the costs they impose upon society, such as reduction in quality of water flowing from their forests. Forest industry firms, as all private business, must earn a return on invested capital and, if possible, some profits in addition. Their actions may be limited by the capital or the credit sources available to them. But all of these problems are not peculiar to forest industry business; they exist for all business.

The American public has a right to expect the forest industry to be efficient in the private business sense of the term, as it has a right to expect every private sphere of activity to be efficient. By and large, the industry firms that own forests are efficient growers and processors of wood. Although efficiency in the private profit sense of the term is a highly desirable, even necessary, attribute of any industry, this alone does not guarantee that its actions are wholly in the general public interest. Sometimes, indeed, efficiency in the private profit sense leads to actions harmful to the public—noxious substances discharged to air or water, for example. If the general public wants some kind of forestry other than that which is most profitable to the firms concerned, then it must either provide economic incentives for the desired kind of forestry, or it must pass laws and establish rules and regulations for forestry on the private lands. Unless or until society as a whole, presumably operating through the national government, does take effective action to induce or to require some forestry measure, then mere oratory is useless.

## OPERATIONAL OR ADMINISTRATIVE PRACTICALITY, AS APPLIED TO SMALL PRIVATE FORESTS

The small private forest owner faces all the operational or administrative problems of the large forest industry forest owner and much more besides. He cannot capture some of the values his forest management creates, such as watershed and wildlife, any more than can the large forest industry forest owner. He may encounter difficulty capturing the recreation benefits even when he owns the forest primarily for its recreation values. Small landowners—"second home" owners generally—often experience trespass and damage to their property because they are not in residence all the time. But, beyond these problems of forestry common to all private forest owners, the small private forest owner faces peculiar and difficult operational or administrative problems.

First of all, the small private forest owner often lacks a clear understanding of his objectives in forest ownership or tries to hold mutually inconsistent objectives. Does he seek the place primarily for its recreation value to himself and his family? Or does he expect or hope for an increase in land value when he sells the property? Or is he primarily concerned with income from wood production? Over how long a period should he plan to maximize whatever it is he seeks to maximize? He often will state one set of objectives yet actually act as if a different set were guiding him. Not knowing where he is trying to go, he naturally has some difficulty getting there.

Secondly, the small private forest owner frequently lacks the knowledge and the skill to understand the physical and biological limitations and possibilities of his forest and to analyze the economic efficiencies of various possible lines of forest operations, nor does he know where to acquire the necessary technical and administrative knowledge. He may suspect, and often he would be right, that acquisition and use of the necessary knowledge and expertise would not reward him commensurately with the effort that would be required. For him, the management problems are not worth worrying about—let the forest grow as it will, sell the standing trees or the land when it best fits his personal needs for cash, and accept the results as inevitable or tolerable. For many small private forests, the difference in annual income between low level and high level management is less than $1,000, and to secure this gain he would have to invest significant time, thought, and managerial skill.

But, thirdly, even the small private forest owner who did know what he sought from his forest and was able to plan and to decide rationally and wisely, would often have great difficulty in carrying out his forest production decisions. For the great majority of small private forest owners, it would be hopelessly uneconomic to try to maintain his own year-round work force and the necessary equipment. The small private forest owner may be able to hire men or to contract for some operations on a seasonal or casual basis, but such a labor force or contractors are often locally unavailable when needed. All in all, the small private forest owner faces a difficult time in implementing his forest management decisions.

Lastly, the small private forest owner often markets his wood output badly. Someone approaches him with an offer to buy all the merchantable trees from his tract; he often decides to accept (or to reject) this one offer without seeking other bids. His personal need for cash may dominate his decision rather than any silvicultural considerations. The buyer is often the operator of a small portable sawmill; he sets his mill up on the property, cuts every tree he thinks he can run through his saw, and leaves the forest in a sadly depleted state. Such mills often cannot produce the maximum value from the wood they process. The mill operator may have made no unreasonable profit, even though he paid less for the wood than it was worth.

To some extent, the marketing problems of the small private forest owner are within his own capacity to solve. There are a very few simple rules that would greatly increase the income he can get from his wood production: always get more than one bid, always mark the trees to be cut (and the stumps, so that checking on performance is possible), always specify harvesting practices, always require advance payment or bond for performance, and, if possible, get professional forester help in as many of these steps as possible. In some situations, it is not possible for the small private forest owner to market his wood to good advantage because there is no buyer, or only one buyer, or there may be so much other wood available on buyers' terms that he cannot obtain any better terms.

Many forest management programs, though technically feasible and economically efficient, simply cannot or will not be carried out on small private forests for the reasons outlined. Various public programs have been aimed at the small private forest owner for some years, but their total effect has been modest. Different public programs, or larger programs of the types used thus far, might help.

Trees will grow on nearly all these forests, and some wood will be produced, regardless (or in spite of) anything that the owner or the public might do. The test of public assistance programs is, will they grow more wood than will grow naturally, and will the added wood be produced at reasonable cost?

A somewhat different approach to the small private forests might pay off better. Instead of, or in addition to, extending technical and financial help directly to the small forest owner for his continued management of the forest, as in the past, the public programs might take the form of financial help in leasing his forest to some manager who could operate a larger and much more efficient forest unit. The owner could retain many rights, including the right of personal use and to increased land values, and the lessee would determine the forestry practices. The income from forest production would be shared between the owner and the lessee. The latter might be a forest consultant, of whom there are getting to be many, or a cooperative, or a unit of local government (a county), or some land management district, such as a watershed association or a soil conservation district. While the problems of arrangements such as this would be great, the possibilities are intriguing. With a great production potential in the small private forests and with a modest output under present arrangements, some new approach to the problem might offer an attractive alternative.

## OPERATIONAL OR ADMINISTRATIVE PRACTICALITY, AS APPLIED TO NATIONAL FORESTS

The operational or administrative problems of national forests are very great, and they are different in many respects from those of private forests. Other publicly owned forests, whether federal or state, face some of the same problems as do national forests. We will consider only the national forests, since they are the largest single type of public forest and, in a sense, a prototype of all publicly owned forests. With slightly over half of all the standing softwood sawtimber in the United States, their very size makes the national forests important, and in the past, administration of the national forests often led the way in the development of good forest practices.

Our general conclusion may well be stated at the outset: there is the gravest danger that the operational or administrative capability of government as a whole, as applied to national forest management, will prove insufficient to realize the physical and economic possibilities of these forests in the future. To point to this problem does not in the least mean that it is insoluble; it may merely mean that greater effort and/or new directions are needed.

The grave operational and administrative problems of the national forests arise from several sources. Each is serious enough, but the combination is so serious as to perhaps be fatal.

### Allocating Forest Uses

The national forests have too many "owners," with divergent views as to how the forests should be used. That is, the national forests belong to all the people of the United States, but some people are in a better position to use them than are others. Some take far more interest in national forest management than do others. Diverse ownership alone would not necessarily mean indecisive decision making; after all, General Motors and American Telephone and Telegraph companies have millions of owners, yet are able to reach firm and reasonably consistent management decisions.

The national forests, like all public lands, are governed by legislation but the legislation is typically vague and unclear, relying on such vague words or phrases as "multiple use," "sustained yield," and others. They are accepted by various interest groups precisely because they are vague—exactly defined words, phrases, goals, objectives, procedures, and other aspects of forest policy would be rejected by too many persons or interest groups to be acceptable. But the vague words and phrases provide no real guide to public officials in the executive and legislative branches when the inevitable conflicts over specific forest management actions arise. Management of public forests is as indecisive in its way as is that of the small private forest owner who does not know what his objectives are.

This problem is surely exacerbated by the unwillingness of many user groups on national forests to assume full financial responsibility for the use they seek; they are unwilling to pay a reasonable market price for the goods or services they get, or to pay the costs incured by the Forest Service in providing these goods and services. As we have noted, only the buyers of wood pay a price which approximates market values (this ignores grazing and some other uses of forest land but not of the forest). Recreation, wilderness, wildlife, watershed, and other uses or values typically cost little or nothing for what they offer users of the national forests. I do not in the least argue that payment of full market prices would simply and immediately resolve all conflicts over national forest administration, because many such conflicts would still persist. But the absence of charges for many uses and values is an open invitation to the assertion of unreasonable demands.

*Budgeting National Forest Activities*

The decision-making process for the national forests has many participants. Some persons seem to believe that management of the national forests is wholly in the hands of the Forest Service. While it is the agency most directly involved and often the only agency at the actual field or forest level of operations, yet in fact many of the decisions about national forest management are made by governmental bodies outside of the Forest Service. The Forest Service must operate within the terms of basic legislation. Such legislation is framed in the Congress, where it is considered by the committees which have legislative jurisdiction over the agency programs. If passed by Congress, legislation must have the approval of the President, unless it can be passed over his veto, and this means approval of the Office of Management and Budget (OMB) as an arm of the President, and usually of the Department of Agriculture (USDA) as the department within which the Forest Service is located, as well as of the Forest Service itself. The respective roles of these various parties is not always easily ascertainable, especially by an outsider. They operate to a considerable degree within the confidentiality of the government processes—even the Congressional committees— and there is undoubtedly a considerable tugging and pulling, a yielding and a resisting, on important matters of legislation. But, all too often, agreement to the degree necessary to get something—anything—adopted means resort to the language of vagueness, and the resulting agreement is on the lowest level of common interest or understanding, or something close to it. Innovation, experimentation, daring, and other actions not in the common mold are discouraged by the process itself.

This multiplicity of factors finds its most concrete and serious expression in the budgeting and appropriation process. The Forest Service is responsible for preparing its budget estimates, as are other federal agencies for their programs. The Forest Service has long employed procedures to measure its work load, using estimated demands from the public for goods and services from the national forests, estimated work needs as defined by the service itself, and accepted work load standards to translate demands into labor force and funds required. Its estimate of work load is one basis of its budget requests each year. One may expect, however, that the agency takes its experience in getting appropriations in the past into account; if appropriations for some kinds of activities have been somewhere near the desired level and have been far short of this level for other activities, the experience can hardly help but affect the requests of the agency for funds for the next year. There are many reasons why a federal agency hesitates to seek, year after year, either appropriations or legislation which it has reason to believe it cannot or will not get. Thus, the Forest Service's original budget estimates are a mixture of what it believes is really needed to do the job it thinks must be done on the national forests, and of what it thinks it can or might actually receive. The outsider cannot know the proportions of these two influences in the final budget figure. Perhaps the Forest Service itself would be hard pressed to estimate the exact weight it gives to these two different factors, each of which affects its budget estimate. It is significant that some of the conservation organizations have undertaken legal action to force the budgeting process into the public arena.

If these conflicting pressures were the sole source of vagueness in the budgeting and appropriation process for national forest management, it would be serious enough, but this is only the beginning of the process. The service develops its budget estimates each year under the guidance of a "ceiling" figure provided by the USDA (Secretary's Office), which in turn is based upon a ceiling provided by the OMB. A departmental figure is presumably arrived at by consideration of the totality of all federal expenditures in relation to federal revenues and by the policy of the President as to a balanced or unbalanced budget; the agency figure reflects in part, competition among bureaus in the department. As such, expenditures for national forest management (as for other federal resource programs) compete with expenditures for governmental services of all kinds. As we have noted, there is no capital account—capital investments are treated as if they were current outlays; there is no charge for past investment nor for the capital tied up in the timber stands of the national forests. There is a tendency to postpone expenditures, such as replanting, because it is mistakenly believed they can be postponed without serious consequence. At any rate, the ceiling figure is a guide, often a directive, to the Forest Service as to its total requested budget. Although budget requests in excess of the ceiling are not permitted by OMB, it does accept appeals for individual items in excess of the ceiling; but the federal official making such a request feels about like a batter with two strikes against him and a fast-breaking curve ball coming down the channel.

The Forest Service's initial budget request is subject to review at the department level and the departmental budget is reviewed by OMB. These reviews, which examine the reasons for changes and even the extent of the changes, are typically conducted in administrative confidentiality. An outsider may, if he is skillful enough, have a fair idea as to the total effect of such review in a given year, but not as to the reasons why or the specifics of actions. Finally, the President's budget goes to the Congress, with specific sums for specific purposes for national forest management. Congressional committees can either increase or pare this budget, and all too often they have passed the appropriation tardily, after the beginning of the year to which it applies. An appropriation, once passed, becomes a firm guide to Forest Service expenditures during the year; sums explicitly provided for one purpose cannot be diverted to another (except for some fire-fighting expenditures).

The results of this process for fiscal 1972 are illustrated in table 15. The appropriation for national forest management for the preceding fiscal year had been about $370 million. The Forest Service asked for increases totalling about $84 million. Its requests involved an increase in every item shown in this table, but a great deal of the increase was for construction and land acquisition, with other substantial increases for forest revegetation and for recreation. The Department of Agriculture in this year denied virtually all the increases and in a few cases cut below the preceding year appropriations. The OMB restored a substantial part of the departmental cuts, though not all of them, and in a few instances made small increases above the Forest Service requests, and Congress appropriated slightly more than OMB had approved, especially for land acquisition, construction, and reforestation. In this particular year, the big bad boys of OMB and of Congress were more generous to the national forests than the USDA family was.

Some of the expenditures are directly comparable with some items of receipts but many are not. More than half of the entire appropriation was for control of fire and insects and for essentially capital investment, such as land acquisition, construction, and road building. Control of fire, disease, and insects clearly benefits wood growing and later harvest, but some of the fire hazard has been caused by recreationists and other users, and they benefit to some extent from a healthy forest—they would generally regard a fire-blackened or insect-killed forest as culturally unacceptable to them. Likewise, the roads are often designed to get timber out of the forest but usually have substantial utility to, and use by, recreationists and other general users.

The overwhelming source of revenues from national forest management is timber sale—all other sources produce less than 6 percent of the total revenue. If all the protection and construction costs are added to the timber management costs, there was a cash deficit in this fiscal year from timber management and growing; if some of the protection and construction costs are charged to other users, then

Table 15. Budget Estimates, Appropriations, and Revenues from National Forests, by Function, Fiscal 1972

(millions of dollars)

| Function | 1971 Appropriation | 1972 Fiscal year budget and appropriation | | | | |
|---|---|---|---|---|---|---|
| | | Forest Service request | USDA request | OMB approval | Appropriation | Revenues |
| Appropriated Funds: | | | | | | |
| Recreation and public use | $ 37.3 | $ 47.4 | $ 38.1 | $ 40.1 | $ 40.3 | $ 7.5 |
| Wildlife habitats | 4.9 | 6.5 | 5.4 | 6.2 | 6.2 | 0.0 |
| Water, incl. power | 10.5 | 16.6 | 12.5 | 13.0 | 13.3 | 0.2 |
| Range management and improvement | 15.1 | 17.1 | 15.2 | 15.4 | 15.4 | 4.9 |
| Land classification and use | 7.2 | 8.6 | 7.4 | 7.4 | 7.4 | 1.1 |
| Mineral claims and leases | 5.1 | 6.9 | 5.2 | 5.1 | 5.4 | 5.0 |
| Timber management and sales[a] | 75.8 | 95.7 | 78.6 | 91.5 | 96.0 | 321.0 |
| Fire, insect, disease control | 50.1 | 53.3 | 49.1 | 49.5 | 49.6 | 0.0 |
| Construction, land acquisition, roads | 164.9 | 203.1 | 161.3 | 196.8 | 206.8 | 0.0 |
| Subtotal | 370.9 | 455.2 | 372.8 | 435.0 | 440.4 | 339.7 |

[a] Includes reforestation.

timber may have produced a cash surplus in this fiscal year. If only expenditures for timber management, timber sales, and reforestation are considered, then timber produced a substantial excess revenue over sales. In any case, these are not really profit and loss considerations, since much of the expenditure is for investment, not for current operations alone; but, on the other hand, this cash account includes no charges for past investment or for interest on present value of the timber stands, nor does it consider changes in inventory values.

In this fiscal year, activities of the national forests other than timber harvest produced vastly less revenue than the funds expended directly on their management. Recreation, wildlife, water, and range management each produced less than a third of the direct expenditures on them, and if some share of the protection and construction expenditures were charged to these uses, the gap would be greater. Had recreation or wildlife produced more revenue, would the various actors in the appropriation process have been willing to ask for, approve, and appropriate more funds for these activities? It may or may not be significant that for the first five items in table 15 (recreation, wildlife, water, range, and land), as a whole, the Forest Service got 36 percent of its requested increases, while for the last three items of appropriation (timber, protection, and construction), as a whole, it got 100 percent of the increase requested. Had the Forest Service asked for all it really wanted for the first five items, rather than (probably) tempering its requests by its judgment of their probable success, the contrast would have been even sharper.

This comparison strongly suggests that revenue production from the national forests does indeed influence appropriations for their management. If this is true, then perhaps the conservationists as a group should seriously reconsider their traditional opposition to some form of national forest management in which expenditures could be somewhat related to, if not directly proportional to, revenues from the same activities. They have feared domination of national forest management by the revenue producing activities, but perhaps ways could be found to create safeguards against such domination. Based upon experience in the last two decades, the choice seems to be between inadequate funds, which are unrelated to revenues, and more nearly adequate funds, based to some degree on revenues.

A contemplation of table 15 raises again some of the questions of economic efficiency. Are total expenditures on national forest management reasonable in view of the output from such forests? A more rational answer to this question would be possible if table 15 were truly an income, expense, and investment tabulation, that is, if all outputs of the forest were valued at their full economic worth, if allowances were made for additions to inventory, and if charges were made for capital. In 1971 cash revenues were about 10 percent less than cash expenditures. Very rough calculations suggest that a true income account (which included a generous allowance for the value of services not now sold at full value prices) would show a substantially larger deficit, largely because interest charges on the value of the national forests would be so large. If this is true, what are the economic and social justifications of public ownership and management of forests, which produce a large deficit by reasonable accounting standards? Are the management costs excessive, either because of some inefficiencies in management, or because inappropriate levels of management are chosen? If the full value of some services, such as recreation, are not great enough to match the costs of providing those services, on what economic or social grounds does one defend them? In my judgment, this type of economic analysis very much needs to be made; the time and information available to me have not thus far made it possible to make such an analysis, and in any event a full economic analysis is the subject for another publication.

As it now operates, the appropriation process for federal forest land management is much more a political than an economic process. The various actors in the process recommend or approve expenditures based on their concepts of need or value without comparing these sums directly with the economic values that they may create. In this respect, the appropriations for federal forest land management are not unlike the appropriations for various welfare programs. Some of the forest users have not liked the results; my contention is that the results have been a direct consequence of the process. If we want different results, then we must consider and strive for different processes.

*Measuring the value of national forest output*

Economic calculations or economic efficiency have either not been made or have not been decisive in national forest management. There are difficult problems in measuring the values of products and services created by national forest management that are not sold in a competitive market, and in trying to capture some of these values. But there have been few funds available to make such measurements and little encouragement to the Forest Service to undertake the measurement of the values created or for their capture. There have been almost no economic calculations as to the optimum amount of timber inventory to carry on the national forests; inventory has been treated as a silvicultural problem. There has been little economic analysis of the optimum investment in tree planting, timber stand improvement, road construction, and other investment on national forests. The kind of data we presented in chapter 7 on returns from different forest practices have come out of the research branches of the Forest Service, but there is little evidence that such calculations have governed national forest administration. There has been little economic analysis of the comparative efficiency of management of site classes, and such studies as have been made seem not to have been used in administration.

It is exceedingly difficult for an economist to visualize what can adequately substitute for economic analysis in decisions about what combination of national forest outputs to produce, what combination and what level of inputs of productive factors to use, in determining the optimum investment levels, the optimum rate of new investment, and the like. To the economist, there is only one common unit of measure of such diverse factors and forces—the monetary unit. If ecologists, silviculturalists, wilderness lovers, or any other group concerned with national forest management have any other method of analysis or any other common unit for comparison, this has not been evident from their writings. Thus far, neither economists nor any other professional group has devised fully satisfactory methods of measuring all these factors. In the absence of some method of analysis and of some unit of measure, management decisions necessarily have a fuzziness and an inconclusiveness which cannot but affect the actual management of the forests.

*Management conservatism*

Bureaucratic and professional inertia and resistance have certainly affected national forest management. Some of these are in federal agencies other than the Forest Service; for instance, OMB seems to have approached national forest financing with much bureaucratic rigidity. Some of these bureaucratic and professional rigidities are common to all government; it is always easier to play it safe, to take as few chances as possible, to evade responsibility for decision or action which may encounter criticism, to avoid taking unpleasant or difficult actions for the purpose of increasing operating efficiency, and so on. Some of this, indeed, pervades all large organizations, private as well as public. Many foresters in public employment today are highly conservative in their forest policy. They emphasize long-range planning, for the forest takes decades to grow to maturity, and their management, which results in very large forest inventory, is costly today to society as a whole. The emphasis on very slow harvesting of the mature old growth timber is one example. The *Forest Service Manual* still uses a 100- to 150-year conversion period for old growth timber; this means some of the trees will be 200 to 300-or-more years old when harvested (if they survive) and that inventory will be very high throughout nearly all of this long period. A conservatism in national forest management which was socially advantageous in an earlier day may no longer be so.

National forest administration has lacked the sharp, keen, cutting edge of profit maximization, which has helped forest industry forestry to overcome some of these same inertias and rigidities. Most people inside the Forest Service and outside would reject profit maximization as the overriding goal of national forest administration. But how much economics in national forest management is optimum? Might it be possible to interject a great deal more economics to the actual benefit of the conservation objectives of the friends of the national forests?

A consideration of the foregoing operational or administrative problems of the national forests led to the tentative conclusion stated at the beginning of this section: there is the gravest danger that the operational or administrative capacity of government as a whole (not merely the Forest Service) is insufficient to realize that combination of various forest outputs which is both physically and biologically feasible and economically efficient from national forest management. The problem is not peculiar to any particular presidential administration; it has existed through many presidents and will continue through many more. The severity of the problem may wax and wane as national economic conditions change, but it is persistent. When the wood and other forest outputs of the national forests were much smaller, these operational and administrative deficiencies were not too serious, but they are likely to be very serious in the future.

If the analysis in this subsection is correct, there seem to be four broad national forest policy alternatives for the nation:

1. Accept as inevitable the inadequacies of standard governmental processes as applied to national forest management, in the same way some people accept as inevitable the shortcomings of small private forest management. In this case, operational or administrative practicality sets the ceiling for national forest production, not physical or economic capability. If this approach is chosen, one simply would have to be reconciled to the deficiencies and comparatively low output of the system. Put so baldly, few would choose

this alternative, but in practice specific action to change it might be lacking or insufficient.

2. Improve the present governmental process without basic change in its form or functioning. Undoubtedly, separation of capital and current accounts, sharper economic analysis to provide estimates of values and costs not now counted, and other measures could suggest more efficient ways of managing national forest inventories and lands and could be the basis for budget estimates and for appropriations. Performance at Forest Service, Departmental, Presidential, and Congressional levels might all be improved greatly. Planning, budgeting, appropriations, and expenditures might thus be at or nearer to economically efficient levels, with long-term planning horizons and appropriation carrythroughs to effectuate long-term plans. Efforts in this direction have been made for many years and will likely continue. Will they be sufficiently effective to make a real difference? The very fact that such efforts have been made for many years, with so little result, makes one skeptical about the future.

3. Some major revision in the whole process of national forest management, particularly budgeting and appropriation, might be undertaken. The potentialities of government corporations, such as have been used in this and other countries for management of basically economic enterprises, surely offer one possible line of action. Some way of gearing expenditures to values created, both to limit expenditures when values do not warrant them and to guarantee expenditures when values are sufficiently large, seems essential. Conservation interests have opposed utilization of receipts for timber management, fearing that timber output of national forests would be favored to the disadvantage of other outputs. If the full values from forest outputs other than timber were paid for by users, then some or all of this objection would be removed; or if an automatic appropriation for recreation visits of fifty cents per visit (or some other figure) could be added to whatever sums were actually collected, a fund might be provided for management of nontimber outputs; or various other arrangements could be devised. National forests were an innovative and creative social institution when first conceived; modern defenders and supporters of the national forests must be equally inventive to provide national forest management arrangements adequate to meet modern conditions.

4. If society as a whole, operating through its elected government, is unwilling to provide a mechanism to manage national forests more nearly approaching their physical, biological, economic, and

social capacity, perhaps we should consider selling large acreages of the more productive timber lands to private owners and managers. Large acreages of the less productive timber lands could be preserved for nontimber outputs, expecting that they would cost substantially more for annual management than they returned in annual revenues. So stated, nearly everyone would reject this alternative; yet it is a logical one if collectively we are unable or unwilling to create a system of management for national forests adequate for the times.

# 11.

## Forest Policy Formation in the United States

If an individual or a group seeks to influence forest policy, then he or it must understand how forest policy is now formed, and how it might be formed. Otherwise, efforts to influence policy are likely to be ineffective or frustrated. By forest policy, I mean all public actions (generally this means actions by government at some level) which significantly affect the use and management of forests, both publicly and privately owned ones. Some actions or measures are directed at forests, while others have different primary objectives but nevertheless affect forests significantly; the line between the direct and indirect measures is obviously neither neat nor sharp. Some measures produce intended effects upon forest use and management, others do not produce the intended or desired effects, while still others have unintentional or unplanned or unexpected results. As with many other aspects of modern life, it is often impossible *not* to have a policy; that is, the decision to do nothing about some situation may be as important and as effective a policy as any line of action that could have been devised. "Policy" surely connotes some major degree of purpose—an intent, a conscious consideration with a chosen answer, even when the answer is to do nothing.

MAJOR FOREST POLICY AREAS

Although a considerable number of public measures might qualify as "policies" in the above sense of the term, the major ones affecting forests are as follows:

1. *Taxation.* Since forests usually involve high investment in standing timber during much of the growth cycle and sometimes other large investments, and since the rate of turnover in this investment is low, taxes are often a major cost of private forest ownership and production for all outputs of the forest. Federal income tax provisions governing the degree to which some items of cost, such

as tree planting, may be "expensed" or charged off against current year's operations rather than included as a capital investment are highly important. So is the ability to include part of the income from sale of forest products as capital gains, rather than as ordinary income. Local real estate taxes are often a major cost in forest ownership, and the way such taxes are levied may make a great deal of difference to profitability of forest ownership.

2. *Foreign trade.* The imposition of import duties or tariffs or the imposition of quotas on imports of wood products surely may affect the supply of wood products, hence their prices. This group of public policies chiefly affects wood growing. The imposition of export controls on forest products would have an effect, perhaps a major one, on the returns from forest ownership and hence upon forest management. Beyond these measures, which are directly applicable to forest products, trade policy in general, including the need to stimulate exports and/or reduce imports to improve an adverse balance of payments, may have a significant effect on forest profits and management for wood production.

3. *Housing programs* greatly affect the demand for wood products, hence the prices of these products, and this has numerous further effects upon forest ownership and management. The volume of housing construction depends in considerable part upon the general economic health of the country, as well as constituting one major element which determines that health. The state of the general money market, or the amount of mortgage credit available and its price, has a major influence on the volume of housing construction. The amount of subsidized housing, if any, also affects the volume of construction activity and hence the demand for wood products.

4. *Transportation.* Wood produced in the forests must be transported to consumers, who often are located a long distance away. Forest products can be shipped economically by water from Alaska or the Pacific Northwest to Japan but not to the Atlantic Coast because of the high intranational freight rates sustained by the Jones Act. Railroads in the United States suffer from a general malaise; their rates are moderately high, at least for some products, and their continued availability may be critical to some forest management.

5. *Direct aids* to forestry have included research, education, fire prevention and fire control, disease and insect control, and subsidized inputs such as seedlings for planting.

6. *Administration of public forests*, including appropriation of funds, is highly important in the United States. Although more than half of the standing softwood sawtimber is on national forests, national forests are also actively in demand for many forest uses other

than wood growing. National policy for national forests includes such matters as withdrawing some forest areas from harvest for conservation reasons, establishment of wilderness areas, methods of timber harvest (including clearcutting), charges made for the various nonwood outputs of the forest, level of appropriations, methods and rate of harvesting old growth timber, determination of optimum volume of timber stand inventory, and others.

## IMPORTANCE OF FOREST POLICY

Forest policy is important for various reasons, including the fact that forests themselves are important in American life and that forests have long been the object of public policy in the United States. It is impossible to escape public action on the foregoing matters of public policy—whatever is done will have some impact.

The ramifications of forest policy are wide. That is, public actions will affect not only forest landowners and forest users, but will have wider effects as well. In particular, the supply of wood in its various forms will have some impact upon the volumes of substitute building materials that will be required. Although wood and the various metals have many uses unique to each, wood (including paper) can substitute for metals and vice versa for a considerable range of uses. One must, therefore, consider the environmental impacts of wood and of alternative building materials when forest policy is reviewed. Likewise, the possibility of recreation within forest settings will affect the demand for other types of land for recreation use.

## FOREST POLICY FORMATION NOW

At the present time, the formation of forest policy in the United States is fragmented and diffuse. Forest policy formation for each of the policy issues is a complex process with many actors, each having some role, but none having a dominant role, and sometimes operating in contradictory or nullifying ways. In addition, many considerations other than forestry affect forest policy decisions; for instance, forest policy with respect to foreign trade may be determined by other international considerations, or federal forestry programs may be dominated by general budgetary and fiscal conditions, almost irrespective of forestry situations. It is unrealistic, and perhaps undesirable, that forest policy for the whole nation should be made by any single agency or group, but questions may well be raised as to the wisdom of the highly diffused policy process now existent.

The Forest Service plays a major role in the formation of national policy with respect to forests. An old, able, and respected federal agency, it is charged by law with the collection, analysis, and publication of data on forest area, timber stand, wood growth and harvest, utilization of forest products, and related matters. In addition, it is the management agency for the national forests and has legal responsibility for an extensive program of cooperative forestry with the states. Each of these roles is obviously important, but the Forest Service does not have final responsibility in any of these roles; its authority and its responsibility are shared with the Department of Agriculture, the Office of Management and Budget, and, of course, with the Congress. The Forest Service has long taken policy positions on many forest issues within its field of responsibility and it surely is influential on those issues. There is reason to believe that it is less powerful today than it once was—not because of a loss in its own competence, but because of the rising influence of many other organizations both public and private.

Other federal land managing agencies, such as the Bureau of Land Management, Fish and Wildlife Service, National Park Service, Department of Defense, have important but lesser roles in the formation of national policy for forests. Likewise, a number of state agencies have various roles to play in the management of state-owned land and in working with private forest landowners.

Congress plays a significant role in authorizing legislation or appropriations for federal programs, including programs for cooperation with states and with private landowners. Its capacity to legislate and to appropriate is severely hedged by the role of the Executive Branch but is none the less real.

The forest industry clearly and reasonably plays a role in forest policy formation. As the business group most directly concerned with forests, the forest industry and its representatives seek to prevent public actions harmful to their interests and to promote actions helpful to them. Because of their considerable economic stake in the nature of public forest policy, the industry can afford to spend substantial sums to obtain and to analyze information; not infrequently, its representatives are better informed than are the representatives of any other group. Although the industry does not command a large block of votes, its economic power is substantial. Its lobbyists, like lobbyists of many other business groups, are often highly effective because they are alertly on the job at all times.

The numerous conservation organizations have a proper concern with national forest policy affecting both private and public forests. Their members are users of forests for various purposes. The conservation organizations often have very definite ideas about how forests should be managed and used—ideas which are, to a considerable extent, independent of the economics of the situation, but ideas which they will strive vigorously to see implemented. For most conservation organizations, forestry is only one interest. The organizations, as such, have access to their members, and in recent years their access to the information media of the country has been very good. By informing various people of their attitudes, they have been able to influence many people and, through them, to influence public officials even though their economic stake has been low and even though they have assumed little or none of the costs of their positions—other than the costs any taxpayer bears. On the whole, the conservation organizations cannot afford to be as well staffed as can the forestry groups; able people in their headquarters offices are often spread very thin and are unable to specialize in forestry matters.

Lastly, there is the "public"—the great mass of the electorate, often not well informed about forestry, often largely indifferent to it, with little direct stake in forest policy that its members can easily see, and yet extremely powerful if some issue is simple enough and dramatic enough to command its attention and support. In the past twenty years or so, for instance, state after state has passed bond issues to buy substantial acreages of land, forested and nonforested, for additions to the state parks. A majority of the voters were sufficiently interested in such cases to vote for measures which they knew would cost them taxes, but which they supported for the values created thereby. When the general public turns out to use forested areas for outdoor recreation in ever mounting numbers, public officials are forced to take measures to accommodate the crowds. Sooner or later, public attitudes are likely to be translated into legislation.

These various interest groups could have been subdivided much further. The interests of the various groups sometimes coincide, in which cases informal alliances may be formed or the actions of one group reinforce those of another; sometimes their interests differ, and actions are taken by one group which may compete with, or nullify, those of other groups. The alliances and rivalries are not wholly constant but to some extent vary from issue to issue. Sometimes a particular group, such as an industry or conservation group, speaks with essentially one voice—its members are all or nearly all in agreement on some issue—but sometimes a group has substantial difference within its ranks. Then it may have trouble arriving at a position or in pursuing some course vigorously.

## WEAKNESSES OF THE PRESENT POLICY-FORMING PROCESS

Implicit in the foregoing description of the policy-forming process for forests in the United States are some criticisms. First of all, there is no organization to look at all forests in all their uses and in all their aspects. Forest policy is an incidental objective or purpose of many organizations; it commands neither the full time nor the full attention of the ablest men. The input on forest policy from many organizations, both public and private, is relatively small in many cases and often overlooked as forest policies are actually formed. In short, it is a weak policy-forming process.

It may be argued that the Forest Service is the central policy making body for forestry in the United States. Perhaps this was true once, but it does not seem to be so today. True, the Forest Service has many men of ability, and it does devote significant resources to studies of policy implications and to direct policy making efforts, but in the language of World War II, it is a "claimant agency"—it has its own objectives, criteria, and interests, and as a result the other public and private organizations are unwilling to concede it an over-all leadership or dominant role. Its power and responsibility are particularly marked for the national forests and for forestry research of all kinds, but other agencies also exercise power and have responsibility here. The Forest Service has a more limited influence over the vast number and area of small private forests because the owners of such forests respond to many influences. The Forest Service's influence over the forest industry is still less. No one, of course, can deny that the agency has these powers and responsibilities, and no one should ask that it refrain from using them. Its role in the formation of forest policy for the nation, defining the latter in the broadest possible terms, is less easily measured but is surely only one of many influences. The issue is: Is the Forest Service power and responsibility as a forest policy forming body sufficient to fairly describe it as dominant? Or is it merely influential? My judgment is that the latter is more accurate.

It might equally be argued that the Office of Management and Budget is the dominant agency in forming forest policy for the United States. It clearly has the power to direct and to override the Forest Service and other federal land managing agencies. However, its role in forest policy is largely negative, is incidental to its many other duties, and is not accessible to the public.

A second criticism of forest policy formation is that the really significant issues in U.S. forest policy are either not raised at all or are raised in too narrow a framework. A few illustrations help support this position. The desirable level of appropriations for federal forest land managing agencies is looked at in a narrow framework of the effect of expenditures upon the federal budget. Output and income from management programs are considered only to a limited extent, and the long-run consequences of forest production at half or less of potential capacity enters into the consideration little or not at all; or the issue of clearcutting forests is looked at primarily as an aesthetic insult—which it usually is—without real consideration of whether some areas should be cut at all or not, or what the alternatives are if the area is cut; or exports of logs to Japan are opposed without consideration of balance of payments effects or of whether prohibition of exports would actually increase domestic lumber supply at all. In all too many instances, the full range of relevant considerations is not brought into the discussion nor are all the significant alternatives explored. The result is that second-rate or worse choices are made.

As a result of these shortcomings, one must say that much forest policy in the United States is inadvertent and inadequate. The sum of a considerable number of separate, independent actions taken for specific rather narrow purposes simply does not add up to a comprehensive, imaginative, constructive national policy.

## POSSIBILITY FOR IMPROVEMENT IN FOREST POLICY FORMATION

If one is dissatisfied with the present forest policy processes in the United States, what are the alternatives? The range of alternatives listed near the end of chapter 10, where appropriations for national forest management were discussed, are relevant here also. One might simply accept the present policy forming process, with all its idiosyncrasies and deficiencies, as inevitable, unchangeable, a cross one has to bear to obtain the other values of a democracy; or one might seek to improve the functioning of this process without in any way changing its basic structure; or one might seek some wholly different approach.

In any event, it would be helpful if there were some better forum than now exists, in which issues of forest policy could be raised and debated. There is a need for more facts—more dependable and relevant ones—but above all there is a need for a process by which all relevant alternatives could be explored and debated. There is perhaps no lack of debate today, but its quality could be improved greatly so that less time was spent in arguing about trivial or incidental issues.

Decisions about public actions must always be hammered out in the political process. This involves the President, the Congress, and the voters. Professional and technical people can assemble data, make analyses, and propose alternatives, but they rarely can, and should not, make the final policy decisions. However, the political process could be more informed and wiser than it has been.

It was considerations such as the foregoing which led the President's Panel on Timber and the Environment to propose the creation of a new and special forest policy board. This board was proposed as advisory to the President. It was felt that such a board could have no influence or power other than what the President would give it. If he followed its advice, its influence would be great; if he habitually disregarded it, its influence would be nil—and its legal charter would make no difference either way. The proposed board was to have citizen, not public employee, members. The functions of the board were visualized as constant review of the forest situation, analyses of relevant data, and formulation of recommendations for specific policies for the President and, through him, for the nation. "The Panel is not so naive as to assume that national policy for forests can be formulated, considered, and adopted in any single place; but it does believe that the scattered threads of forest policy could be drawn together better than they are today, if this were the explicit and sole task of some organization."[1]

No single measure, including any suggested by the Panel, can insure an ideal forest policy—however that may be defined. Alternatives surely exist and will be preferable to some groups. The essential consideration, in my scale of values, is that forest policy for the nation (including policy for the national forests) be considered more carefully, more innovatively, more consciously, and by a wider range of interest groups than has been the case until now.

[1] Report of the President's Advisory Panel on Timber and the Environment. (Washington: Government Printing Office), Apr. 1, 1973, p. 116.

# 12.

## One Man's Conclusions on Forest Policy Issues

In chapter 2, we listed seven presently pressing issues of forest policy in the United States: (1) how much land to devote to forests, (2) how much forest land to withdraw from timber harvest, (3) by what methods to harvest the timber that is harvested, (4) how best to manage the national forests, and in particular how best to harvest the mature old growth timber found on many of them, (5) how to economically increase the output from the numerous small private forests, (6) what environmental constraints should be placed on timber growing and timber harvest, and (7) what constraints, if any, should be placed on foreign trade in forest products. We pointed out that these seven issues overlapped to a degree, and that other issues could also have been listed. But these, we think, pretty well cover the forest policy field in the United States today.

Chapters 3 through 11 presented some relevant facts, bearing upon these policy issues and a schema or method for analysis of forest policy issues. We found that an adequate consideration of policy issues in any natural resource field involves at least five separate factors: physical feasibility and consequences, economic efficiency, economic welfare or equity, social or cultural acceptability, and operational or administrative practicality.

This approach does not lead to neat and tidy answers. Those who regard economic efficiency as the sole criterion for forest policy are horrified at the loose structure of this approach, at its inability to arrive at a single answer, and at its inability to measure quantitatively the difference between one "solution" and another. This approach requires five kinds of facts; it involves five types of approach or analysis. It is almost impossible to maximize five factors simultaneously, hence any solution involves at least four factors at less than their separate maximum stages. But it was argued in chapter 3 —and we reassert it here—that this approach is far more realistic than any simpler one. Any simpler approach will be short of reality, as this is found in policy debates and actions, and will prove unacceptable to at least some of the participants.

Having made this type of analysis and having presented some facts in the foregoing chapters, what do I conclude about a desirable forest policy for the United States today? Any reader of earlier chapters will surely have gotten some hints of my position but now I will make my conclusions explicit. Others might not agree with my conclusions even if they accept my schema for analysis and accept my facts: they might weight the same facts differently, particularly because their concepts of cultural acceptability are different from mine, or they might introduce additional facts into the analysis.

## HOW MUCH LAND TO DEVOTE TO FORESTS

This general issue breaks down into two parts: How much effort, if any, should be directed to preservation in forest uses of presently forested areas? What efforts, if any, should be directed to restoring or developing forest cover on land capable of commercial forest tree growth but now lacking any trees or lacking a reasonably satisfactory stand of trees?

On the issue of preserving presently forested land in forests, my answer is: expend no efforts in this direction. The acreages of forest land likely to be diverted from forestry to nonforestry uses are small compared with the total forest area. The need for forest land is not so acute as to require the preservation in forests of all land capable of growing commercial trees, and the difficulties of trying to protect forest land from conversion to nonforest uses are so great as to make the results not worthwhile. There are other ways—more intensive production from better sites, in particular—to get any needed output of forest services of any type (not merely more wood). Arguing that society should not expend any significant effort to retain in forestry all land now in forests does not in the least argue that society should not control the other uses of land which might develop on land that is presently forested. In particular, the high-pressure, high-promotional development of vacation or second homes on forest (and other) land has environmental, economic, and social consequences sufficiently grave to warrant social controls over this type of land conversion—but not for the purpose of preserving the land in forests.

On the issue of restoring or improving the tree cover on potential forest land now unstocked or understocked, my answer is: yes and no. Yes, for the most productive forest sites; no, for the least productive commercial forest sites. Here, as elsewhere in this book, I use the Forest Service site productivity classification because I have no other. It utilizes physical criteria only (cubic feet wood growth per acre annually); an economic classification would be preferable. Yes, restocking or improved stocking is desirable for land in site classes I through III, or generally for better forest sites where trees will grow relatively rapidly and where the wood has significant value. For more mediocre forest sites, site class IV generally, mostly let nature take its course. Such sites will reforest naturally, though slowly; the first tree crop may be a poor one, but ecological succession will generally work to restore original forest types. If sites can be replanted cheaply, and if the resulting wood can be cheaply harvested—circumstances which apply to some site class IV pine lands in the South—replanting may be economic on these below average sites. For the poorest forest areas, site class V generally, reseeding and replanting is usually simply not worth the cost. Not only should little or no public funds be spent to replant or to improve forest cover on public forests of this site class, but they should not be spent, as a general rule, for replanting similar lands in private ownership. If private land owners wish to invest in stand regeneration or improvement on such poor sites, that is, of course, their privilege, but they should be warned that the income prospects are not good.

I hasten to point out that there will be exceptions to the broad conclusions stated in the foregoing paragraphs. For instance, there may be a particularly fine stand of some species of trees relatively near some city and often used and admired by many people, which should be saved from harvest or from land conversion to other uses; there may be some tract of land on which tree growth will be slow because soils are thin or for some other reason, where replanting is worthwhile because of its suitability for recreation use even if very costly in terms of wood production; early restoration of some type of plant cover on bare land may be desirable to reduce soil erosion; some sites, classified rather low on the productivity scale using physical criteria only, may have economic prospects good enough to warrant spending money on their replanting, or drainage or fertilization might economically raise the classification of a site; a particular tract of relatively poor forest land may be planted as part of a planting operation which includes a much larger surrounding area of higher site quality. Other exceptions could be cited, but the general conclusions stand.

## HOW MUCH COMMERCIAL FOREST LAND TO WITHDRAW FROM TIMBER HARVEST

The amount and location of commercial forest land to withdraw from all timber harvest depends upon the purpose of the withdrawal, the productivity site classification of the land, its ownership, and whether the land is now covered with merchantable timber or whether the tree cover must be restored. The purpose of the withdrawal may be to conserve the soil against undue erosion, to preserve some scenic value, to make the area available for relatively intensive or developed recreation, to preserve some watershed value, to protect wildlife, for some scientific value, or as wilderness area. Harvest may be foregone in some instances because forest regeneration of the site is doubtful. Productivity site classification is perhaps the most important factor of all in considering which lands to withdraw from timber harvest; the loss of income from withdrawing low productivity sites is relatively small, while the loss of monetary income from not harvesting high productivity sites is large. When a site has presently merchantable timber, in volume and of quality which warrant harvesting, and where the costs of harvest are less than the value of the timber, then withdrawal means some loss of immediate income; withdrawal from future harvest of a site recently harvested or denuded by fire or storm means a loss of future income. Publicly owned forests may more appropriately be withdrawn to secure nonmonetary values than many privately owned forests; the private landowner will be less inclined to take into account values which he cannot realize but which accrue to others. All of these points have been made in earlier chapters, but may now be applied more specifically.

I would withdraw publicly owned commercial forests of low productivity site class that are now forested from timber harvest relatively generously for all the purposes mentioned in the foregoing paragraph. I would couple my willingness to withdraw such merchantable stands of timber with a program to grow wood more intensively on the more productive sites. In making withdrawals for soil conservation, watershed preservation, wildlife protection, and other similar conservation purposes, I would recognize that the line between withdrawal and harvest is not always easy to draw, and that it is affected by technology and care in timber harvest. I would recognize also that the method of timber harvest (selective, shelterwood, clearcut, or other) would have some effect upon the decision to withdraw for some reasons but not for others. Roads can be built to lie lightly on the land, logs can be removed by "walk-lightly" methods, under some conditions trees can be left to protect water from adverse effects, and other measures can reduce environmental impacts. Moreover, I would temper my withdrawal of these less productive sites by some consideration of their extent in relation to productive forest sites. For instance, in the Pacific Northwest more forest land lies in high productivity classes, hence one could withdraw most of the less productive sites; whereas in the Black Hills of South Dakota one would have little forest land left for harvest if all the lower productive sites were withdrawn from harvest.

On publicly owned commercial forests of low site productivity, where the once existent timber stand has been harvested, I would expend little money to restore the stand and would not expect to harvest the site for another 100 to 200 years, if ever. This position could usually rest solidly on the economics of timber growing on such sites. Such sites might be used for other forest outputs or uses.

On publicly owned commercial forests on the more productive sites, whether there now existed a stand of merchantable timber or whether restoration of a stand was the forestry problem, I would withdraw land from timber harvest sparingly. Most such land would pose only mild conservation problems due to timber harvest, hence withdrawals for this purpose need not be extensive. Since the economic values from timber growing and timber harvest are higher on the more productive sites, I would apply economic criteria to the use of such forests more strictly than for the less productive forests where the economic values are low in any case.

Withdrawals of forest land for wilderness purposes do not differ conceptually from withdrawals from timber harvest for any other purpose. In each case, there should be a clear definition of the purposes of the withdrawal, a measurement of the gains from withdrawal and from harvest, and a delimitation of the appropriate area. But wilderness is an issue of so much popular concern that it seems essential to make a few comments directly about it. I would withdraw public forest lands of low site productivity generously and would withdraw lands of higher productivity more sparingly. These are intentionally somewhat imprecise terms, which would have to be applied explicitly in any given situation. I certainly would not exclude wilderness use from all productive forest sites, but I would count the cost of withdrawals on these sites. I would not apply economic analysis too strictly to the establishment of wilderness areas; I would favor a few areas which had some wilderness appeal even if it could be proven, or merely argued persuasively, that their economic value was higher for timber growth and harvest. My position here is thoroughly inconsistent, and I cannot be pushed too far; to some modest degree, I am a wilderness advocate, but not one without concern for cost, value, and alternative use of the forest. My willingness to withdraw forest generously for wilderness use is conditional upon the wilderness lovers and the public forest management agencies agreeing upon some means of limiting wilderness use to capacity. If excessive use is to destroy its capacity to provide a wilderness experience, why bother to establish a wilderness?

For privately owned forests, the withdrawal situation is necessarily somewhat different. I assume that the private forest owner, whether large or small, will follow his long-run interests except as restrained by law or by public opinion. Either law or public opinion might well enforce conservation measures on private forests if the consequences of timber harvest had adverse off-site effects. Such constraints might well be on output standards, letting the forest owner meet such standards as best he could. One must assume that private landowners will harvest existing stands of timber if it is profitable, even on the less productive sites. Since many such sites have stands of timber that are not highly profitable to harvest, and since the economics of timber growing on such sites are unattractive, perhaps in some cases such sites might be acquired by a public agency and used for nonharvest forest uses. On the more productive forest sites, where intensive forestry is economic, one would expect private forest owners to make very few withdrawals from timber harvest.

These various considerations can be translated into specific proposals for withdrawal of forest from harvest in many different ways. In table 14, in chapter 7, I presented one "scenario" of forest land management, a low-acreage high-intensity scheme which included consideration of productive site class and forest ownership and which recognized that not all owners would follow the same program even when their lands were similar. That scenario intentionally involved a very high—perhaps a maximum—withdrawal of forest from harvest, and to this extent it was unrealistic. Innumerable possibilities exist to produce more wood than is being grown today and at the same time to withdraw substantial acreages of forest from harvest. A willingness of the various contenders for forest land to search diligently and constructively for mutually acceptable forest management programs should pay off handsomely in terms of constructive results.

HOW TO HARVEST TIMBER

The policy issues are about methods of timber harvest often stated as one issue: opposition to clearcutting. Numerous groups have sought with much energy to outlaw or forbid clearcutting, at least on public forests. However, the issues are a good deal broader than merely clearcutting. To focus entirely on this one method is to miss both the major issues and the best resolution of such issues.

First of all, I would reserve significant areas of commercial forest land from cutting by any method, as outlined in the foregoing section. I do not know how large the acreage so reserved would be because there is an unknown but substantial overlap of areas withdrawn from harvest for conservation, recreation, wilderness, wildlife, watershed, and aesthetic reasons. If the reservations from harvest were very generous, they could possibly be as much as a fourth of all commercial forest land (including commercial forest in site class V). Whatever the percentage of commercial forest areas reserved, the proportion of forest productive capacity reserved from cutting would be less than half as great; this is inherent in the classification of forest land by site class. If my conclusions about reservation of commercial forest land from cutting were followed, and if my conclusions about environmental protections are also followed, many of the more controversial cutting situations which have arisen in the past would be eliminated.

Secondly, what is the purpose of any timber harvest, by any method? If the purpose is merely to get out the merchantable timber in the cheapest possible way—and that is often the purpose of the buyer of timber from a small private owner—then sometimes the cheapest method is clearcutting, but more often the cheapest way is a poor type of selective cutting. The logger frequently takes all the trees that he thinks he can run through his saw and return wages or better, and he takes few pains to preserve the stems he does not take. Where there is a mixture of species, he takes the more valuable ones, leaving the less valuable ones to capture the site. The result may be a tree cover remaining on the ground, but the true forest has been destroyed. Clearcutting under these circumstances would have been more costly, but the forest which naturally became established after such a harvest would have been an ecologically and economically more productive one. This process of selective cutting, or something close to it, has created some millions of acres of mediocre to worse hardwood stands throughout the eastern half of the United States. Clearcutting for economic reasons may also leave an area equally poorly equipped for reproduction, as well as aesthetically offensive during the regeneration period. The degree of skill with which any method is employed may be high or low.

If timber harvest is viewed as an indispensable tool in forest management and in tree growth, then the method of timber harvest should be selected with management objectives in mind. For most forests, renewed tree cover, continued tree growth, and preservation of the basic productive capacity of the forest ecosystem will be among the management objectives. If these are the objectives, then the characteristics of the site become all important. The method of timber harvest may be selective cut, or shelterwood cut, or clearcut, or some other form with equal appropriateness under different conditions. Where there is a forest of mixed ages, as ponderosa pine generally is, or of both mixed ages and mixed species, as many eastern hardwood types are, then a cut selecting among trees on the basis of size, age, thrift, and perhaps species is often the indispensable forest management tool for that site. For some of the warmer and drier sites for Douglas fir, especially on the eastern and southern edges of the Douglas fir belt, shelterwood cutting, whereby one cut takes some mature trees but others are left for some years for seed and ground shelter and removed later, may be the best method of timber harvest. For some sites and species, clearcutting to expose mineral soils for new seedlings to root in and to provide sunlight is indispensable. For a badly degraded mixed hardwood site, the only way that desirable species and desirable trees can be reestablished within less than a few generations may be to remove all existent trees—clearcut—and start over. A lodgepole pine site, of even-aged but overmature trees, heavily infested with dwarf mistletoe, must be clearcut if a clean new stand is to be reestablished. For this latter situation, no cutting at all may be the most economic forest management if the site is very low in productivity, or if natural regeneration is uncertain and slow. In short, the competent forester who seeks to manage his forest for continued high level wood production must use the most appropriate method of timber harvest as an indispensable management tool.

The method of timber harvest has special characteristics in mature old growth forests. As a matter of fact, most such forests are part of the national forests and are mostly some type of pine or of Douglas fir. Some of the trees in such stands have died and some have fallen; there is much defective wood in the standing live trees as well as on the ground. Any method of harvest which removes only that wood which can be economically removed will leave large volumes of defective wood behind. It is more obvious on a clearcut site; it is partly concealed on a selective cut site. Where wood chips have significant value for paper manufacture, it is economic to remove more of the wood that is defective for purposes of lumber manufacture than where no such outlets exist, but in any case some wood so defective it is valueless for any purpose is likely to remain. Such defective materials can be, and generally should be, removed for aesthetic and other reasons by piling and burning.

Timber harvest by any means may be aesthetically offensive, but by proper care can be far less so. Clearcutting is always a shock, ecologically and aesthetically. But the extent of the shock can be reduced by more care in laying out the harvest area, by disposal of slash and waste, and by prompt regeneration.

When considering the policy issues of methods of timber harvest, it is essential that the full physical-biological and economic potential of intensive forestry be kept in mind. If most of the nation's wood were grown on the better forest sites under economically sound intensive forestry methods, tree harvest would come from a much smaller total land area than if all so-called commercial forests are cut, but a given tract of forest would be cut much more frequently than is the case now. After the initial harvest, there would be far less defective material in subsequent harvests. Each harvested tract would get back into tree growing more promptly than now. More of the total forested area would not be cut at all or would be cut only very infrequently. The whole regimen of tree growth, tree harvest, and stand regeneration would be very different from that today, both for the intensively managed sites and for the least intensively managed areas.

NATIONAL FOREST MANAGEMENT

The national forests include a very large area of land with many diverse natural resources and with many diverse demands on those resources; about half their total area is commercial forest (including site class V land). They are administered under a variety of laws including the Multiple Use and Sustained Yield Act of 1960. There are many policy issues, and hence many controversies, about the best management of these lands. The focus in this section is on the problems of managing the mature old growth timber stands, and their ultimate conversion to a rotation of growth and cut.

A few brief facts may be cited again, to set the stage for my conclusions about management of these timber stands. The national forests (including site class V land) contain slightly more than half of all the standing softwood sawtimber in the United States; their inventory of both standing sawtimber and standing total timber per acre is by far the highest of any major type of forest land ownership; their rate of annual wood growth—whether expressed as cubic feet per acre, as a percentage of the volume of standing timber, or as a percentage of their potential capacity—is the lowest of any major type of forest land ownership. They are an immense storehouse of mature, somewhat defective, nearly nongrowing timber, and there is a great annual loss of dead and decaying timber. As an economist, I am shocked at the immense inventory value of the standing timber on national forests and at its very slow growth rate. This is hardly productive in the physical or economic sense. In their own way, these forests are as unproductive as bare potential forest sites.

Even with generous reservation of national forests for wilderness and other nonharvest uses, the harvest of old growth timber on national forests should be substantially accelerated above present rates. In a mature forest, harvest inevitably exceeds net growth, whether or not it exceeds long-term sustained yield, and an accelerated harvest on national forests for the next two decades would almost certainly be well above net wood growth in those years. However, growth would rise considerably as old growth areas were harvested, assuming that intensive forestry were followed on the better sites. I would aim to reduce the inventory of standing timber on national forests; I think it is excessive from a purely silvicultural viewpoint, and it is grossly excessive from an economic viewpoint. If the national forests are ever to grow more timber, at a rate more closely approaching their potential, then more timber must first be cut from them. It would be possible to accelerate their timber harvest greatly while remaining within the principle of sustained yield. The President's Advisory Panel on Timber and the Environment concluded that the idea of even flow of timber products, which the Forest Service has added to the 1960 Multiple Use and Sustained Yield Act, should be abandoned.

An acceleration of the cut of old growth timber on national forests would undoubtedly pose many difficult technical problems, and some economic ones as well. But the most serious problems would be cultural acceptability. The 100-year-and-longer conversion of mature old growth specified in the Forest Service *Manual* would have to be changed. To many persons, foresters and nonforesters, inside and outside the Forest Service, a marked acceleration of cut of old growth timber will be a traumatic experience. Nevertheless, if the national forests are to produce as much as they are reasonably capable of producing, their management must be changed in the future. We nonforesters have a right to ask foresters to work out and to implement a program of national forest management that is more economically productive and more attuned to the needs of our times. One aspect of such management must be more intensive management of the lands used for timber production. This requires greater expenditures, hence larger appropriations and better assurance of continued adequate support.

OUTPUT FROM SMALL PRIVATE FORESTS

I must confess to some uncertainty or even ambivalence about the small private forests. The nature of my uncertainty will be clearer if we review some of the more outstanding facts about these forests.

The "other" private forests (those not owned by the forest industry) include nearly 60 percent of the entire forested area of the United States. While a few owners have some thousands of acres of land, most such ownerships have only a few hundred acres or less. Many of these ownerships include land of lower site quality, but on the whole they average almost as high in productivity as all other forests taken as a whole but considerably lower than forest industry forests. In 1970, the other private forests were more lightly stocked with growing trees than was any other major type of forest ownership, but their net growth rate per acre was above average and was almost double the admittedly low net growth rate on national forests. Harvest in 1970 was substantially below growth, so that inventory of standing timber was being built up.

An on-the-ground inspection of many of these forests will show that the present timber stand has been badly degraded by past harvests of the type previously described. In addition to having a light volume, these stands often include poorer species or poorer individual trees. Observations of the management of such small forests will often show that the periodic harvests are poorly planned and conducted, both in terms of what is done to the remaining timber stand and in terms of economic returns to the owner. It is often said that the owners of these small forests lack technical knowledge about how to manage them better, and that one of their needs is for technical advice and assistance.

As I contemplate the statistical record of these small private forest owners as a group, I cannot but wonder: Is their accomplishment really so bad given the circumstances under which they must operate? They may attain a comparatively low output from their forests, but they also expend little on them. They surely have not overinvested in timber stand! They may be poor foresters, but possibly they are as good forest economists as are their advisers. I personally feel unquiet with our present knowledge, or our present ignorance, about the operations of this large and diverse group of forest owners.

As long as the rain falls and the sun shines, these small private forests (whatever their site class) will produce some wood, which can be harvested at intervals. The issues revolve around attempts to increase their output over that which would occur "naturally." Public and private programs (other than fire protection) to this end have been rather unrewarding in the past. But I agree, somewhat reluctantly, that present public and private programs aimed at increasing the output of the small private forests should be continued. I would also try the new approach to the problem described in chapter 10, under which a system of leasing land from small owners to form larger management units would be subsidized by federal grants, and I feel intuitively that there must be other approaches which would be rewarding.

If it is culturally and politically acceptable to do so, I would limit both public and private programs for these forests to those on the average or better forest sites, to those of the average or larger acreages per ownership unit, and to those producing wood for which there is an active demand. Certainly, greater returns per unit of expenditure will be achieved in this way. But a program limited to the larger and better situated private forest owners might seem elitist or discriminatory to some people, even when greater wood output per unit of cost was admitted.

ENVIRONMENTAL POLICY ISSUES INVOLVING FORESTS

The environmental policy issues involving forests fall into two rather distinct categories: those involving forests as one of several other sources of raw materials and those within forestry itself.

Wood is a versatile and valuable raw material, used throughout the world today and used throughout history. Among its many other good features, it is renewable—it grows—and it is biodegradable when no longer needed in its original purpose. The fuel requirements of wood manufacture are generally far less than those for alternative raw materials. In a world which is becoming increasingly environment and energy conscious, wood has a great many advantages.

In thus urging more extensive use of wood, I most certainly do not condone any and all forestry practices, regardless of their environmental impact. Nor do I accept a greater use of wood as an excuse for not instituting greater environmental protection and conservation for fuels and metals. Nor do I accept greater use of wood as a justification for every use of wood, fuel, and metals. I personally feel, for instance, that the modern American daily and Sunday newspaper is a disgrace, environmentally and intellectually, and I would favor means to reduce newsprint consumption. Similarly, some forms of consumption of metals and energy may be socially undesirable and should be or will have to be curtailed in the years and decades ahead. But, for many forms of consumption which will continue, wood fibers in some product form or another are technically and economically good substitutes for the metals (and indirectly for fuels). Environmental concerns will almost surely lead to greater relative use of wood in the future.

Within forestry, clearly greater attention must be paid in the future to environmental impacts than has been paid in the past. The method of timber harvest is particularly important, but environmental protection measures are not limited to timber harvest methodology. Road locations, construction standards, and mileages are highly important, regardless of whether the roads are used for timber harvest or for recreation; in many areas, 90 percent or more of the accelerated erosion associated with timber harvest has come from roads, not from the other logging operations. Greater attention will also have to be directed to preservation of water quality in streams and lakes, to preservation and care of wildlife generally, and to forest aesthetics. Without necessarily endorsing everything which is advanced in the name of environment, I nevertheless agree that all uses of forests in the future must pay more attention to environment than they have in the past.

The real question is: How is this desired result to be attained? Presumably stricter environmental controls can be imposed on publicly owned forests, for environmental considerations have too often been neglected on them in the past. The requirement for environmental impact statements and the possibility of citizen suits to enforce this process may bring desired changes; but is this the efficient way to attain this goal? How can more attention to environmental considerations be required on private forests? Education of forest owners and managers and of timber harvesters, and enlistment of their cooperation, are essential, but are likely to be insufficient. I shrink from the complexities and ramifications of laws which closely control forest operations on private land. But how else does one deal with the forest owner or timber harvester who resists any other approach?

As the reader can easily see, I am fairly confident as to ends but dubious as to means for greater environmental concerns in forestry.


POLICY ISSUES IN EXPORTS OF FOREST PRODUCTS

The only significant policy issue with respect to foreign trade in forest products relates to log exports to Japan. Imports of lumber from western Canada, imports of hardwood plywood from Japan and elsewhere in the Pacific, imports of newsprint from eastern Canada, exports of paper and paperboard to Europe from the southeastern United States, and exports of wood chips from the Pacific Northwest to Japan have raised no serious policy issues—at least not thus far.

I fully support not only continued, but expanded, export of logs to Japan. The argument that this export reduces domestic supply of wood is nonsense. If the Japanese were cut off from U.S. log exports, they would buy lumber in the United States or Canada—unwillingly, but most probably to about the same volume as they now buy logs—and hence U.S. supply of lumber would not be increased significantly, if at all, by a cessation of log exports. While log export increases competition for logs in the Pacific Northwest, I see no good reason for sheltering such firms from competition. Log export may slightly increase wood prices in the United States, but I do not regard this as a serious problem. I would *increase* log export over a period of years. With the increased harvest of old growth timber on national forests and with increased wood growth on forests of all ownerships, this would be perfectly possible without seriously disrupting current domestic supply. More importantly, if the United States is going to continue to import some of the metals and other raw materials it needs, and to import the manufactured products it wants and can get cheaper by importing, then we must export something. We have priced ourselves out of the international export markets for many industrial products, but our natural resources and our productive manpower and management enable us to compete very well in world markets for farm commodities and forest products. The conservationists should be reminded that when we export logs and import metals we trade an environmental impact in our forests, which by careful management can be very small, for an environmental impact in mining and refining, which may be great.

Unequivocal support for long-run substantial log export is not incompatible with suggesting that there may be times when the Japanese might appropriately be urged by our government "to cool it." The demand for lumber in this country for building construction fluctuates violently so that sharp rises in lumber prices, followed by almost equally sharp declines, take place at intervals. If the Japanese should expand their log buying, in order to expand their housing construction, at the same time as domestic demand was rising sharply to expand our housing output—and this is exactly what happened in late 1972—then a difficult supply-demand situation is exacerbated, and appeals for legislation to control log exports increase. The Japanese, given the nature of their economy and the role of government in that economy, could surely find a way to step up their log buying when U.S. demand for lumber was weak and to decrease it when U.S. demand was high. Over a period of years they could buy a large amount of timber in the United States with a minimum amount of disturbance to our markets.

# Bibliography

Barney, D., *The Last Stand*. New York: Grossman, 1974.

Bolle, A., *A University View of the Forest Service*. Washington: USGPO 90–115, 1970.

Clawson, Marion and Burnell Held, *The Federal Lands*. Baltimore: Johns Hopkins, 1957. See also the update of this by Clawson, *The Federal Lands Since 1956*. Baltimore: Johns Hopkins, 1967.

Clawson, Marion and Jack Knetsch, *The Economics of Outdoor Recreation*. Baltimore: Johns Hopkins, 1966.

Clawson, Marion, ed., *Forest Policy for the Future*. Baltimore: Johns Hopkins, 1974.

Clepper, Henry, *Professional Forestry in the United States*. Baltimore: Johns Hopkins, 1971.

Conklin, J., "New Forests of New York," *Land Economics* (May 1966).

Duerr, W., D. Teeguarden, S. Guttenburg, N. Christiansen, eds., *Forest Resource Management*. Corvallis, Oregon: OSU Book Stores, Ind., 1974.

Duerr, William A., ed., *Timber!* Ames, Iowa: Iowa State Univ. Press, 1973.

Frome, M., *The Forest Service*. New York: Praeger, 1971.

Gates, Paul, *History of Public Land Law Development*. Washington: USGPO, 1968.

Greeley, W. B., *Forests and Men*. Garden City: Doubleday, 1951.

Gregory, G. R., *Forest Resource Economics*. New York: Ronald Press, 1972.

Horwitz, Eleanor, *Clearcutting: A View from the Top*. Washington: Acropolis Books, Ltd., 1974.

Johnston, D. R., A. J. Grayson, R. T. Bradley, *Forest Planning*. London: Faber and Faber, 1967.

Kaufman, Herbert, *The Forest Ranger*. Baltimore: Johns Hopkins, 1967.

Nienaber, J. and A. Wildavsky, *The Budgeting and Evaluation of Federal Recreation Programs*. New York: Basic Books, 1973.

Osborn, W., *The Paper Plantation*. New York: Grossman, 1974.

President's Advisory Panel on Timber and the Environment, *Report*. Washington: USGPO, 1973.

Schiff, A. L., *Fire and Water*. Cambridge: Harvard Univ. Press, 1962.

Smith, David M., *The Practice of Silviculture*. New York: Wiley, 1962.

Spurr, Stephen and Burton Barnes, *Forest Ecology*. New York: Ronald Press, 1973.

USDA Forest Service, *Environmental Program for the Future*. Washington: USFS, 1974.

USDA Forest Service, *The Outlook for Timber in the United States.* Forest Resource Report 20, Washington: USGPO, 1973.

USDA Forest Service, *The Principle Laws Relating to Forest Service Activities.* Agriculture Handbook No. 453, Washington: USGPO, 1974.

USDI Bureau of Outdoor Recreation, *Outdoor Recreation: Legacy for America.* Washington: USGPO, 1973. See also the separate Appendix "A" to *Legacy for America.*

U.S. Public Land Law Review Commission, *One Third of the Nation's Land.* Washington: USGPO, 1970.

Vaux, Henry J., "How Much Land Do We Need for Timber Growing?" *Journal of Forestry* (July, 1973).

Weyerhauser Corporation, *The Potential for Tree Improvement.* Centralia, Wash.: Weyerhauser Corp., 1971.

Wood, N., *Clearcut.* Sierra Club Battlebook, San Francisco: Sierra Club, 1971.

Worrell, Albert, *Principles of Forest Policy.* New York: McGraw-Hill, 1970.

Worrell, Albert, "What Can We Expect Private Forests to Produce?" *Journal of Forestry* (December 1969).

# Index

**Library of Congress Cataloging in Publication Data**

Clawson, Marion, 1905–
  Forests for whom and for what?

  Bibliography: p. 171–172
  Includes index.
  1.  United States—Forest policy.  2.  Forests
and forestry—United States.  I.  Resources for the

Future.  II.  Title.
SD565.C58       333.7′5′0973      74–24399
ISBN  0–8018–1698–X (hardcover)
ISBN  0–8018–1751–X (paperback)